The
IMPOVERISHED
GASTRONOME

David Chater was for many years a sub-editor on various financial journals. From his North London home, which he shares with his wife and young daughter, he travels everywhere by bike. This is his first book.

The
IMPOVERISHED
GASTRONOME

DAVID CHATER

FOURTH ESTATE • *London*

For GILLIAN O'CONNOR.

You couldn't hope to be sacked by a nicer person.

First published in Great Britain in 1996 by Fourth Estate Limited
6 Salem Road London, W2 4BU

Copyright © 1996 by David Chater

The right of David Chater to be identified as the
author of this work has been asserted by him in accordance
with the Copyright, Designs and Patents Act 1988.

A catalogue record for this book is available from the British Library.

ISBN 1–85702–522–9

Typeset by Palimpsest Book Production Limited,
Polmont, Stirlingshire
Printed in Great Britain by Clays Ltd, St Ives Plc

CONTENTS

PREFACE

What happened was that I was sacked.

I'd just started a job at the *Investors Chronicle* and managed to demonstrate a truly remarkable degree of incompetence in a very short space of time. Until quite recently, they used a publishing system based on galleys rather than computers, so there were hundreds of pieces of paper flying in all directions, from the design studio to the photocopying machine to the typesetters down the City Road, many of them passing through my eager little hands. By the time I'd been there a week, very few of the pieces of paper were ending up in the right place and the few that *did* end up in the right place certainly weren't there at the right time. Chaos reigned. The magazine had been around for almost a century, and the editor felt – quite reasonably – that if it was to continue into the next century, it would be much safer to dispense with my services.

But getting sacked leaves a vacuum, especially if you have a wife, a young child, an old dog and a mortgage. In such circumstances, you grab on to certainties. I enjoy cooking – that was one certainty. And I didn't have any money. That was another. So I decided to compile a cookery book for people in the same situation – a sort of mean cuisine.

The idea is simple enough. A fast-food hamburger and chips costs almost £4 a head. It leaves you feeling hungry, full of grease and misanthropy. So I asked a variety of London chefs if they could come up with recipes for a meal – a starter, a main course and a dessert – that would feed half a dozen people for somewhere in the region of a tenner all told, a fraction of the price. A meal that would leave everyone feeling well-fed and at peace with the world.

In the process, I discovered a number of curious things. Chefs are an unimaginably pleasant group of people. They work cruel

1

hours in dreadful conditions for very little money. But tantrums and saucepan-throwing were notable by their absence. I met many chefs who were terminally exhausted, but not a single primadonna.

The other fascinating thing was seeing the relationship between a chef and his food – 'You are what you eat' became 'You are what you cook.' Cooking is as revealing as handwriting.

Finally, it can actually help to be broke. Herring roe, polenta, neck of lamb, stinging nettles, pigeons – these aren't the kind of things likely to be found on too many shopping lists in Harrods Food Hall. But a perfect fishcake argues strongly that being broke, like being hungry, can serve as a strong sauce.

Note: all recipes serve 6 people.

VERY FRENCH

BELGO NOORD

Belgo Noord is a theme restaurant opposite the Round House in Chalk Farm, and as such it has a self-conscious, wow, look-at-me feel to it. You walk through a heavy door and enter the realm of the Deeply Groovy. It's somewhere between a ship and a monastery. You cross a nautical gangplank above the kitchen, where down below the chefs are working away in front of stoves whose chimneys curl up and around each other like gross intestines. The waiters are dressed in the habits of Belgian monks: young men in plum-coloured robes with shaven heads and tiny pigtails, like advertising folk on a religious retreat. The tables are refectory wooden, and right the way around the room, carved into the walls, are words roughly translated from Rabelais: 'Coldeel', 'Thornbach', 'Gurnard', 'Rumblegut' and 'Begginbag'. The food is very good, the bill is very small and the place is very busy.

And the chef, Philippe Blaise, is yet another of these remarkable young Frenchmen bursting with energy and joie de vivre, like champagne on legs, exploding with friendliness and love of food. Like the mustard, he comes from Dijon.

SHRIMP CROQUETTES

1 CARROT	75g (3oz) BUTTER
½ LEEK	SALT AND
1 SMALL ONION	FRESHLY GROUND
½ CELERY STALK	BLACK PEPPER
700g (1½lb) SHRIMPS	GRATED NUTMEG
1 TABLESPOON	2–3 EGGS (OR 1 EGG
OLIVE OIL	AND A COFFEE-CUP
1 TABLESPOON	OF MILK)
TOMATO PURÉE	150g (5oz)
750ml (1¼ PINTS)	BREADCRUMBS
WATER	1 TABLESPOON
125g (4oz) FLOUR	BRANDY (OPTIONAL)

Dice the vegetables and sweat them with the shrimps in the oil for 3 minutes. Add the tomato purée and stir, cooking until the mixture takes on a slightly brownish hue – about 5 minutes. Then add the water, bring to the boil and cook gently for 3–4 minutes. Strain through a colander, retaining the liquid. Process the shrimps and vegetables, then force them through a sieve using the back of a wooden spoon to get rid of nasty, crunchy bits of shrimp carcass.

Make a roux with 75g (3oz) of the flour, the butter and the shrimp liquid, and add the shrimp mixture. Taste for seasoning. Cook until it's almost boiling. Stir in the brandy if desired, and spread on a flat baking tray. You should have a mixture the texture of very thick custard, which will become increasingly solid as it cools. Cut into any shape you like – at Belgo, they use a shape roughly twice the size and thickness of a fish finger.

Beat the eggs – or the egg and the milk. Roll the croquettes into the remaining flour first, then in the egg and the breadcrumbs. Place on a baking tray.

Preheat the oven to 220°C/425°F/gas 8 and cook the croquettes for 20 minutes. Serve with a garnish of a side salad and a wedge of lemon.

ENDIVES PARISIENNE

12 ENDIVES OR
CHICORY
50g (2oz) BUTTER
150ml (5fl oz)
WATER

2 TABLESPOONS
WHITE SUGAR
SALT AND FRESHLY
GROUND BLACK
PEPPER
1 SLICE OF HAM PER
ENDIVE
CHOPPED PARSLEY

FOR THE BÉCHAMEL

125g (4 oz) BUTTER
125g (4 oz) FLOUR
500ml (16fl oz) MILK
75g (3oz) CHEDDAR
CHEESE

SALT AND
FRESHLY GROUND
BLACK PEPPER
NUTMEG

Preheat the oven to 200°C/400°F/gas 6. Put the chicory into a dish with the butter, water, sugar, salt and pepper and bake for an hour. If you want them to stay white, put foil on the top.

Meanwhile make the béchamel: Melt the butter, add the flour and stir on a low heat until it smells biscuity. Then add the milk little by little, stirring all the while to avoid lumps, and stir in the grated cheese and seasoning at the end.

Remove the chicory from the baking dish, allow them to cool, then wrap each one in ham and put in a dish. Smother with the béchamel sauce and place under a hot grill to brown. Garnish with a sprinkling of chopped parsley.

ORANGES POCHÉES AU SIROP

1 ORANGE PER PERSON
750ml (1¼ PINT) WATER
300g (10oz) WHITE SUGAR

MINT LEAVES TO GARNISH (EXTREMELY OPTIONAL)

Carefully remove about half the orange skin, using a zester or a potato peeler. You don't want any of the white pith, so it's a reasonably tricky operation. Then slice the orange skin into matchsticks.

Then, with a very sharp knife, remove the rest of the skin and pith so you're left with pithless and peeled whole oranges.

Allow the water and sugar to boil for a couple of minutes, then add the oranges and cook for 8–10 minutes. Remove and allow to cool.

Simmer the matchsticks of orange peel in about ¾ of a coffee-cup of the syrup for about 45 minutes.

Cut the oranges into thin slices vertically, from top to bottom, and arrange on a plate with a little syrup and a garnish of orange peel. And stick a mint leaf somewhere on the side for good measure. Refrigerate.

FRANÇOIS CLOSSET
BRASSERIE FAUBOURG

It's odd the way people with a fondness for yellow interiors tend to be unusually – remarkably – full of warmth and kindness. The Brasserie Faubourg in Clapham, for example, was a sunny room with yellow walls which François Closset, the chef/proprietor, regularly painted himself.

His father was a chef, his grandfather was a chef, and he was brought up in a kitchen. He cooks with the kind of intuitive ease that comes from a lifetime spent around food. The day I met him, everybody had ignored the set menu and eaten à la carte, which left him with a pile of cold mashed potato. So in the evening, various fortunate residents of south London were offered potato croquettes.

Time and again when he was talking to me, he'd suddenly stop and say: 'Here, I'll show you.' How to arrange a salad, how to properly brulée a crème, what a skirt of beef should look like when it's prepared. Didn't he worry about giving away secrets? 'After Escoffier, there are no secrets,' he said. 'Just a few tricks, which chefs know anyway.' Nicole, his wife, kept gently reminding him that he had to make a terrine for the evening until she finally gave up and went off to collect their son from school.

The menu he suggested was the kind of meal you'd give people you want to feed well rather than show off what a good cook you are. It was horrid to discover suddenly that the Brasserie Faubourg had closed down and there was no listing for François Closset anywhere in London, business or residential.

A SALAD WITH CHICKEN LIVERS

A PACKET OF	OIL
FROZEN CHICKEN	BUTTER
LIVERS	1 GARLIC CLOVE
A SELECTION OF	1 TABLESPOON
LETTUCE LEAVES	CHOPPED PARSLEY
A COUPLE OF	
TABLESPOONS SALAD	
DRESSING	

Drain the livers on thick paper and get rid of any little bits of green nastiness attached to them.

Toss a few salad leaves in a dressing. (Lettuce, oak-leaf and radicchio, for example, or whatever you can find in the market. Most supermarkets do a decent mixed bag of leaves) Arrange them on a plate. There's a trick here which sounds deeply silly, but it works. Hold the leaves in your hand like a small bunch of flowers. Then take any sort of ring or circle – M. Closset just happened to use a 10cm (4in) circle for cutting pastry shapes, although you can improvise one from a bit of cardboard – and pull the bunch of leaves through the ring, letting them fall on the plate. It arranges the leaves and gives them volume. *Voilà*. Instant art.

Sauté the livers gently in oil and butter (more oil than butter) for 5–7 minutes, and at the last minute add a crushed garlic clove and a scattering of chopped parsley. Lay the livers, still hot, on the salad and serve each plate with a couple of slices of French bread, buttered and toasted under the grill.

For the dressing: a little bit of nut oil and a little bit of raspberry vinegar is good if you're lucky enough to have some in your store cupboard.

A variation on this is to pour off the oil and butter, and deglacé the liver in the pan with 1/3 of a coffee-cup of cider vinegar. But if you do this, for gawd's sake don't use raspberry vinegar in the dressing.

SKIRT OF BEEF WITH PROVENÇAL TOMATOES AND POTATO CROQUETTES

FOR THE SKIRT OF BEEF

1.2kg (2½lb) SKIRT OF BEEF
3–4 SHALLOTS, FINELY CHOPPED
1 TABLESPOON OLIVE OIL
A SPLASH OF WHITE WINE VINEGAR
A LITTLE BUTTER
A COUPLE OF SPLASHES OF CHICKEN STOCK
CHOPPED PARSLEY
SALT AND FRESHLY GROUND BLACK PEPPER

Remove the skin from the skirt of beef and slice the beef in half lengthways to make it thinner. Flash-fry the meat and the shallots together in the oil over a high heat for a couple of minutes each side, just like a steak. Pour off excess oil, then deglacé with a splash of white wine vinegar. Then a little butter, a little chicken stock and a scattering of chopped parsley. C'est tout. Absolutement aucune nonsense. Serve immediately on hot plates.

FOR THE PROVENÇAL TOMATOES

6 FAT TOMATOES, CUT IN HALF
SALT AND FRESHLY GROUND BLACK PEPPER
2 TABLESPOONS OLIVE OIL
2 GARLIC CLOVES, CRUSHED
2 TABLESPOONS BREADCRUMBS
A LITTLE BUTTER
CHOPPED PARSLEY

11

Cut the tomatoes in two. Season each tomato with salt and pepper first, then a few drops of olive oil, the garlic, then a healthy little pile of breadcrumbs, and finally a little knob of butter and a sprinkling of parsley and grill until the breadcrumbs are golden.

For the Potato Croquettes

900g (2lb) POTATOES	2 EGGS
300ml (½ PINT)	2 TABLESPOONS
MILK	FLOUR
SALT AND	CHOPPED PARSLEY
FRESHLY GROUND	3 TABLESPOONS
BLACK PEPPER	OLIVE OIL

Boil the potatoes and mash them with the hot milk. Correct the seasoning, and stir in the eggs, flour and parsley.

Heat the oil. Get a scoop of potato the size of a big walnut on a spoon in your left hand, and then – using the thumb of your right hand – drop the potato into the oil and fry on each side until golden. Drain off any excess oil on kitchen paper. You don't have to serve them at once – you can keep them somewhere reasonably warm and revivify them under the grill at the last minute.

CRÈME BRULÉE

2 EGGS	125g (4oz) WHITE
250ml (8fl oz)	SUGAR
WHIPPED DOUBLE	2 OR 3 DROPS
CREAM	VANILLA ESSENCE
125ml (4fl oz) MILK	50g (2oz) SOFT
	BROWN SUGAR

Preheat the oven to 160°C/325°F/gas 3.

Whisk all the ingredients together except the soft brown sugar, and pour into ramekin dishes up to 1cm (½in) or so from the top. Cover each one with silver foil and seal very tightly – use your thumb to press the foil against the lip of the dish, otherwise it'll lift off in the steam.

Lay the dishes in a tray of cool water and cook in the preheated oven for 30 minutes or until they're set. Cool and refrigerate.

Use a knife to ease the brulée away from the edge of dish, then upend each one on to a plate. Rather than putting the sugar on top and sticking them under the grill, melt the sugar in a pan and pour it over.

When eating the brulée, treat the caramelised top as though you were cracking the top of an egg with a spoon – hit it with a sharp tap. The topping is far too hard for digging and scooping to be any good at all.

Interlude de Chavot

I waited for Eric Crouillère-Chavot in an annexe off the main dining-room at the Interlude de Chavot, sitting at a table in front of a huge green plate eighteen inches across. I couldn't see too much of what was happening in the dining-room, but the style of the annexe was Disney baronial, with elaborate cornicing and prints of assorted dukes in plumed hats on the walls. In the distance, I could hear a middle-aged German businessman being pleasant and boring on the subject of chess on the Internet. After half an hour, I wished I'd brought a book.

And then Eric Crouillère-Chavot arrived. Or rather, detonated in front of me. It was like trying to talk to a footballer straight after a match. He was gasping for breath, fizzing with manic energy and trying to focus with all the adrenalin still flushing through his veins. The Eric Cantona of cooking. Ideas and recipes came cascading out of him. He began to describe what he'd cook, and before he'd finished describing one meal, he'd begin to produce a variation on it. Then he'd scrap the whole thing, start off with another, and produce three different ways of doing it with separate sauces. And five alternative ways of presenting it. And then he'd conjure up images of what each one should be served with. This, in turn, would spark off another idea. And just as he was about to finish that one, he'd decide it was all too difficult or expensive for home cooking and start all over again.

It was like watching one of those documentaries of an artist sketching at breakneck speed – lines become shapes that suddenly burst into life. Then the sketch is scrumpled up and thrown away. Someone, you feel, should be scrabbling around on their hands and knees, rescuing them, smoothing them out and filing them away for their grandchildren. It's not surprising all the food guides are throwing stars at him like so much confetti. Nor is it surprising that his recipes are so straightforward, given that the best things are always the simplest.

Finally, a waiter came up and whispered something in his ear. Someone else was waiting to see him. 'Deux minutes!' The waiter murmured again. 'I'm coming. *I'm coming!* They will kill me!'

Being Eric Crouillère-Chavot is an exhausting business.

PEA VELOUTÉ WITH FRESH HERBS

Better known, on this more prosaic side of the channel, as pea soup. Don't be duped into thinking it's dull. It isn't. It's a bona fide, knock 'em dead affair. Grown men have been seen sinking their faces into the soup bowls while making happy gurgling noises.

500ml (16fl oz) CHICKEN OR VEGETABLE STOCK, OR WATER
450g (1lb) FROZEN PEAS
SALT AND FRESHLY GROUND BLACK PEPPER
1 SMALL CARTON DOUBLE CREAM
100g (3½oz) BUTTER
A HANDFUL OF CHOPPED FRESH HERBS (TARRAGON, BASIL OR CHERVIL, OR JUST PLAIN FLAT PARSLEY)
A TRICKLE OF OLIVE OIL

Bring the stock or water to the boil. Add the peas and cook gently for a few minutes. Then liquidise, correct the seasoning and add the cream, butter and herbs with a trickle of olive oil.

CURED SARDINES WITH A SALAD OF NEW POTATOES

6 VERY FRESH,
PLUMP SARDINES
100g (3½oz) ROCK
SALT PER kg (2¼lb)
OF FISH

6 SLICES OF COARSE
COUNTRY BREAD

FOR THE SALAD

450g (1lb) NEW
POTATOES
6 SHALLOTS
2 TABLESPOONS
OLIVE OIL

1 TABLESPOON RED
WINE VINEGAR
SALT AND
FRESHLY GROUND
BLACK PEPPER

Clean and scale the fish, rub them with the rock salt and turn them every hour or so for 12 hours.

Make a little cut in the middle of each tail. Take hold of each side of the tail between thumbs and forefingers – and pull. If the fish is ready and cured, the flesh will peel away from the bone about as effortlessly as skinning a banana. With a sharp knife, lift the flesh off the skin. Toast a few slices of bread and bang the sardines on top.

For the salad, boil the potatoes (you can peel them or not afterwards, depending on how you feel) and mix them with the finely chopped shallots, the oil and vinegar, and correct the seasoning.

PUMPKIN BLINIS WITH A CARAMEL AND RUM SAUCE

1kg (2¼lb) PUMPKIN   SUGAR TO TASTE
FLESH   5 EGGS
100g (3½oz)   1 TABLESPOON RUM
BUTTER

Peel and chop the pumpkin, and put it in a pan with half the butter. Gently fry with the lid on until the flesh collapses – approximately 5 minutes. Then remove the lid, and cook off all the liquid until the flesh is very, very dry. You can put it on a flat tray on a low heat in the oven to dry it out, or hang it in muslin overnight. But come what may, the pumpkin must be dry.

When it's all dried out, let it get cold and purée it. Add 90g (3½oz) of sugar to every 450g (1lb) of pumpkin purée, and mix in 2 egg yolks, one whole egg and the rum.

Meanwhile, whip up 4 egg whites with a pinch of salt until they're stiff, sweetening them at the end with a little sugar to taste. Then fold the egg whites into the pumpkin mixture.

Heat a knob of butter in a frying pan until almost smoking, then drop 1 tablespoon of the mixture into the pan for each blini and cook for a couple of minutes on each side, allowing 4 blinis per person. If you like, you can sprinkle a little sugar on the blinis while you're cooking them – it will caramelise.

To serve, each plate should have a pile of blinis, one on top of the other, with a scoop of vanilla ice cream on top melting pleasantly, surrounded by the rum and caramel sauce.

FOR THE SAUCE

150g (5oz) SUGAR
30ml (1fl oz) WATER
SQUEEZE OF LEMON JUICE
2 TABLESPOONS RUM

Heat the sugar and water carefully, with a squeeze of lemon, until it turns into a golden caramel. Don't let it burn and get bitter.

Pour in a tablespoon of warm rum. When it's cooled down, add an extra teaspoon of rum.

NIGEL DAVIS
BRASSERIE ST QUENTIN

Nigel Davis is another chef who underwent that rite of passage – cooking for two years in France – and loathed it. He's a gentle and curious soul. He produces hundreds of meals a day of classic French cooking in the middle of Knightsbridge, right opposite the Brompton Oratory, and yet he's obsessed with the countryside. One of the reasons he found living in France difficult was not because the French were so unpleasant to him (which they were) but because he missed the English countryside. He loves fishing, but largely as an excuse to don wellies and gulp down oxygen. Everything he catches goes straight back into the river – the only fish he ever caught and subsequently ate was a suicidal trout that he landed three times in a row on the same afternoon.

There's a man who walks into the Brasserie St Quentin for lunch three or four times a week, sits at the bar and eats a veal chop. Always a veal chop. He's known in the kitchen as 'Mr Veal Chop'. Davis dreams of running a small pub somewhere on a river out in the country, where locals who didn't feel like cooking at home could drop by, sit round the bar, and he'd cook for them with whatever fresh ingredients were to hand. He'd get to know the people he was cooking for, and all the Mr Veal Chops would have a first name. And he'd be able to say: 'Sorry mate, the veal chop is off. What about trying such-and-such? If you don't like it, you don't pay for it . . .'

He also gave me an astonishing recipe for armagnac and prune mousse. It has no place in this book because it would almost certainly blast the budget to kingdom come. But not to include it would be an act of criminal negligence. It's pure evil.

AUBERGINE AND RED PEPPER TERRINE

FOR THE TERRINE

4 LARGE
AUBERGINES, PEELED
COARSE SALT (IT
DOESN'T DISSOLVE,
IT JUST DRAWS OUT
THE WATER)
2 LARGE RED
PEPPERS, SKINNED
AND SEEDED

OLIVE OIL
2 EGGS
125ml (4fl oz)
DOUBLE CREAM
CUMIN (WHOLE
SEEDS, ROASTED AND
GROUND)

FOR THE GARNISH

1 SMALL BUNCH OF
PARSLEY
1 GARLIC CLOVE
3 TABLESPOONS
OLIVE OIL

75g (3oz) STONED
BLACK OLIVES
2 ANCHOVY FILLETS
½ BAGUETTE

Cut the aubergines into 6 lengthways. Sprinkle with the salt and leave for half an hour. Gently fry the red peppers in a little olive oil until soft. Drain, allow to cool, and then purée with the eggs and the cream. Put the mixture through a sieve and season with salt.

Wash the salt off the aubergines after they've been draining for half an hour. Pat them dry and sauté in olive oil until lightly browned.

Dip your finger in a bit of olive oil and rub the sides of a terrine, then line it with clingfilm. Assemble the terrine in layers, starting and finishing with the red pepper mixture. Season each layer of aubergine with a liberal sprinkling of cumin.

Preheat the oven to 150°C/300°F/gas 2. Place the terrine in a roasting pan half-full of boiling water and bake for 45 minutes.

To make the garnish, purée the parsley, and garlic with 1 tablespoon of olive oil, and purée the olives and anchovies with 2 tablespoons olive oil. Slice the baguette thinly, spread with the parsley mixture, and bake in a low oven until crisp and brown.

Serve the terrine at room temperature, sliced, and garnish with the bread, spread with a little of the black olive purée.

A Casserole of Ham Hocks and White Beans with Chorizo Sausage

350g (12oz) WHITE HARICOT, LINGOT OR PETIT COCO BEANS, SOAKED FOR 24 HOURS
6 ONIONS
2 HEADS OF GARLIC
FRESH OR DRIED THYME
2 BAY LEAVES

3 HAM HOCKS, SOAKED FOR AT LEAST 24 HOURS IN SEVERAL CHANGES OF WATER
3 CARROTS
3 TOMATOES
2 CHORIZO SAUSAGES
300g (10oz)
225g (8oz) FRESH BREADCRUMBS
OLIVE OIL, FOR DRIZZLING

Cook the soaked beans in water with 3 onions, a head of garlic cut in half, the thyme and the bay leaf, and simmer very gently until the beans

THE IMPOVERISHED GASTRONOME: *Very French*

are almost cooked. How long they take will depend on the age of the beans, but it will be at least half an hour. Don't put in any salt or the beans will harden and never cook. Reserve the liquor and allow to cool.

Simmer the ham hocks in the bean liquor. If necessary, top up with more water. Add more thyme, another bay leaf and the second head of garlic cut in half. Bring to the boil and simmer for 4 hours – until the meat is falling off the bone. Add the carrots and the rest of onions 20 minutes before the end.

Cool the ham hocks, and then take the ham off the bone in healthy chunks. Liquidise a handful of beans with a little of the stock to thicken the sauce. Then transfer everything – ham, beans and vegetables, along with the sliced tomatoes and the chorizo sausages – into a buttered casserole dish, sprinkle with the breadcrumbs, drizzle with a little olive oil and bake in a hot oven until the sauce is bubbling and the breadcrumbs are golden – approximately 20 minutes.

A MOUSSE OF PRUNES AND ARMAGNAC

350g (12oz) STONED PRUNES

100ml (3½fl oz) ARMAGNAC

FOR THE PASTRY CREAM

150ml (5fl oz) MILK
2 DROPS OF VANILLA ESSENCE
2 EGGS

25g (1oz) CASTER SUGAR
15g (½oz) FLOUR

FOR THE CRÈME CHANTILLY

350ml (12fl oz) DOUBLE CREAM
50g (2oz) ICING SUGAR

A DROP OF VANILLA ESSENCE

If the prunes are old, tough and wrinkled, pour hot tea over them and leave them to soak overnight. Drain, then douse with armagnac. The longer you can leave the prunes in armagnac, the better.

To make the pastry cream, heat the milk and vanilla, but don't let it boil. Meanwhile, beat together the egg yolks and the sugar, and stir in the flour.

Pour on the hot milk, whisk, return to the heat and bring to the boil, stirring continuously. Put through a fine sieve and allow to cool.

To make the crème Chantilly, whip together the cream, the icing sugar and a drop of vanilla essence.

Chop half the prunes roughly and purée the other half. Stir in the pastry cream, add the armagnac and fold in the crème Chantilly. Allow to set for 2 hours.

Failing that, here's another recipe for pain perdu, or French toast, on the grounds that you can't have too much of a good thing. If you come across the recipe twice in the same book, you might be prepared to cook it at least once. Repetition, said Goebbels, is the essence of propaganda. My daughter, I discovered, doesn't like French toast. But it's one of those things that children are supposed to enjoy – so just ignore her.

PAIN PERDU

2 EGGS	200ml (7fl oz) MILK
1 BAGUETTE	ICING SUGAR,
50g (2oz) BUTTER	TO DUST

Beat the eggs. Cut the baguette into 1cm (½in) slices at an angle, so you end up with pieces about 12cm (5in) long.

Heat the butter in a frying pan until it's foaming.

Very quickly, dip the bread in the milk – don't let it soak – then turn it in the beaten egg and straight into the foaming butter, and fry on both sides until golden brown. Dust with icing sugar.

THE QUALITY CHOP HOUSE

The Quality Chop House is on Farringdon Road, just down the road from the *Guardian*. For no very good reason, I'd assumed that Charles Fontaine, the chef and proprietor, was a smooth ex-public-schoolboy who'd cornered the market in Olde Englishe Foode – bangers and mash for people in dinner jackets in need of nanny.

Instead, he turned out to be a burly Frenchman who'd spent a year lovingly restoring an old Victorian café to a magnificent state of ecclesiastical discomfort, all dark wood, pews and a big clock. Even if the food was inedible, the place alone would justify a visit. But the food is unpretentious and unadorned, a deeply moral place, open for Sunday brunch.

SPINACH, PEAR AND DILL SOUP

1 ONION
50g (2oz) BUTTER
450g (1lb) SPINACH
2 POTATOES
2 PEARS
2 TEASPOONS CHOPPED DILL
SALT AND FRESHLY GROUND BLACK PEPPER

Soften the onion in the butter, then add the spinach, the diced potatoes, the pears – cored but not peeled – and the dill, along with 1.2 litres (2 pints) of water. Adjust the seasoning, bring to the boil and simmer for 25 minutes and liquidise. In the summer, this soup can be served chilled.

A TERRINE

225g (8oz) CHOPPED
CHICKEN LIVER
450g (1lb) MINCED
PORK
1 SMALL ONION
2 GARLIC CLOVES

2 BAY LEAVES,
ROUGHLY
CRUMBLED
SALT AND
FRESHLY GROUND
BLACK PEPPER

Mix all the ingredients in a terrine, place it in simmering water in a low oven for 2 hours and Bob's ton oncle.

CHOPPED LIVER

1 DICED ONION
450g (1lb) TRIMMED
CHICKEN LIVERS
50g (2oz) BUTTER
3–4 HARD-BOILED
EGGS

A SMALL BUNCH OF
PARSLEY
SALT AND
FRESHLY GROUND
BLACK PEPPER

Gently sauté the onion and the liver (until just pink inside) in the butter. Chop all the ingredients finely, season, press in a container and refrigerate for 5 hours. Serve with matzo biscuits and big gherkins.

GRILLED SARDINES ON TOAST

6 SLICES OF BREAD
6 FRESH SARDINES,
BRUSHED WITH OIL
2 GARLIC CLOVES

2 TOMATOES
SALT AND
FRESHLY GROUND
BLACK PEPPER

Toast the bread and grill the sardines on the same tray. Rub the toast with the crushed garlic cloves, cover with a very thinly sliced layer of tomato, and place the sardines on top. Season.

THE IMPOVERISHED GASTRONOME: *Very French*

LIVER WITH MASHED POTATOES

Few other meals can sound so unprepossessing and taste as good.

5 LARGE POTATOES	1 LARGE ONION
300ml (½ PINT)	1 TABLESPOON
HOT MILK	OLIVE OIL
A KNOB OF BUTTER	½ WINEGLASS
SALT AND	RED WINE
FRESHLY GROUND	1 WINEGLASS
BLACK PEPPER	STRONG STOCK (USE
700g (1½lb)	AN OXO CUBE IF
LAMB'S LIVER	YOU MUST)

Peel and cook the potatoes, and mash them with the milk, butter and seasoning. (Though an infinitely preferable method would be to put them through a mouli, and thence into a processor with the milk, butter and seasoning for 3 short whizzes. The result is light and creamy, a miracle of mashed potato. But leave them in the processor a second too long and you'll end up with glue.) Keep them warm in a low oven.

Slice the liver and cook gently for 3 minutes. Remove from the heat.

Fry the onion in the oil until it's golden brown, add the wine and stock, cook for 5 minutes and return the liver to the pan.

APPLE COMPOTE AND FRENCH TOAST

4 COOKING APPLES
SUGAR TO TASTE
NUTMEG, CINNAMON
OR CLOVES
(OPTIONAL)
6 SLICES
STALE BREAD

300ml (½ PINT)
MILK
3 EGGS, BEATEN
125g (4oz) BUTTER
ICING SUGAR FOR
DUSTING

Peel, core and slice the apples, add sugar to taste and cook slowly until soft. You can add a little nutmeg, a little cinnamon or a small clove if you like. Refrigerate.

Turn the bread in the milk and then in the beaten eggs. Fry in butter like a fritter, dust with icing sugar and serve at the side of the compote.

BRUNO LOUBET
L'ODÉON

There are chefs and there are superchefs. Chefs are people who cook, and superchefs are people who cook while the media watches.

Bruno Loubet is the ultimate superchef – the Ayrton Senna of the kitchen. I arrived at L'Odéon in Regent Street (which is absolutely *the* place, my dear, for a plate of roast lobster) and the place was teeming with cameras and lights and media folk with pigtails wearing mustard-yellow wool jackets, with Bruno Loubet giving Naomi Campbell's mother sound bites to camera.

'Action!'

'And I weel cook for you ze duck een a sauce roquefort,' says the chef.

'Cor, that sounds *smashing*,' squawks Naomi's mum.

'Lovely. *Lovely*,' says the mustard jacket.

You'd expect a published superchef who has dealings with the pigtail brigade to be prattish around the edges. On the contrary, there's a childlike quality to Bruno Loubet that is deeply beguiling: a golden boy, unspoilt, full of laughter, having a glorious time and willing to share his toys. And interestingly, his recipes are about as simple and straightforward as they come.

He sat down, drank an orange juice, then rattled off the recipes in about two and a half minutes flat. 'Is 'ard, you know, the life of ze chef. I cook 180 meals. I do thees, then I do that. For sure I 'ave a 'art attack. You write zat in your book.' And then off he ran again, chuckling away to himself.

PARSNIP SOUP FLAVOURED WITH CURRY

1 LARGE ONION
3 GARLIC CLOVES
A LITTLE OLIVE OIL
1 TABLESPOON
CURRY POWDER
6 MEDIUM PARSNIPS
1.7 LITRES (3 PINTS)
WATER (OR USE
CHICKEN STOCK
AND OMIT THE
STOCK CUBE)

1 CHICKEN
STOCK CUBE
SALT AND
FRESHLY GROUND
BLACK PEPPER
FRESH CORIANDER
TO GARNISH

Sauté the onion and the garlic in a little olive oil until soft. Add the curry powder and the peeled, finely sliced parsnips. Sweat for 5 minutes, making sure there's no discoloration, then add the water and the stock cube or the stock. Bring to the boil and simmer for 45 minutes. Correct the seasoning.

Liquidise, and serve with a garnish of fresh coriander and a dribble of olive oil.

THAI MEATBALLS IN A COCONUT SAUCE

3 GARLIC CLOVES, CHOPPED
2 LIME LEAVES, CHOPPED
1 TEASPOON CHOPPED MINT
1 TABLESPOON CHOPPED CORIANDER
SALT AND FRESHLY GROUND BLACK PEPPER
750g (1½lb) MINCED PORK
1 RED CHILLI, CHOPPED
1 EGG
2 TABLESPOONS OLIVE OR VEGETABLE OIL
1 TIN COCONUT MILK

Finely chop the garlic, herbs and spices, and mix everything (except the oil and the coconut milk) in a bowl.

Fashion 12 meatballs, then fry them briefly in oil to seal them. Transfer them to a saucepan and simmer gently in the coconut milk for 10 minutes.

Serve with rice and garnish with steamed vegetables.

SOFT MERINGUE WITH A FRUIT COULIS

A PINCH OF SALT
8 EGG WHITES
8 TABLESPOONS
CASTER SUGAR
3 KIWI FRUIT
RED FRUIT OF
YOUR CHOICE
(STRAWBERRIES,
RASPBERRIES,
REDCURRANTS,
WHATEVER)
2 SQUEEZES OF
LEMON JUICE

Preheat the oven to 180°C/350°F/gas 4.

Add a pinch of salt to the egg whites and beat until almost stiff. Just before they're stiff, beat in 4 tablespoons of caster sugar and continue whipping.

Pour into 6 small buttered moulds, or 1 large one. Bake in the preheated oven for 3 minutes if they're in small moulds, or 6 minutes if it's a large mould.

Turn out on to a dish.

To make the coulis, liquidise the fruit separately with 2 tablespoons of sugar each and a squeeze of lemon. Pour in alternate dollops around the meringue, and then – for a bit of high-camp ponce – zig-zag a knife through the dollops so they mingle.

Alternatively, you can use the leftover egg yolks to make a crème anglaise instead of the fruit coulis.

Jean-Luc Morcellet
La Dordogne

W alking into La Dordogne in the early afternoon is like entering the chapel of a funeral parlour. The drapes were closed, the lights dim, the atmosphere hushed and heavy with cigar smoke. I imagined, the moment I walked through the door, what Jean-Luc Morcellet would look like. Very pale, with thin lips and bony hands. Bloodshot eyes and a slight tremor . . .

Whereas in fact he was a stocky chain-smoking Frenchman who could easily have bounced straight off the set of *Grease*. Before coming to England, he had worked in vast hotels in Paris and Jerusalem, and then set sail on a luxury cruise liner where he specialised in arranging buffets for 2,000 passengers. He's getting married in six months to a half-Irish, half-Scottish girl in Zimbabwe.

In the meantime, he's finding Chiswick a little dull.

Brandade of Salmon

225g (8oz) FILLET OF SALMON	2 TABLESPOONS CHOPPED CHIVES
2 TABLESPOONS OLIVE OIL	4 DROPS TABASCO
225g (8oz) POTATOES	SALT AND FRESHLY GROUND BLACK PEPPER
2 GARLIC CLOVES	
½ COFFEE-CUP MILK	

F ry the salmon very gently in the olive oil for a minute or so each side, making sure it remains moist and pink inside.

Boil the potatoes in their skins, and when they're ready, peel and dice them roughly.

32

Simmer the garlic whole for 20 minutes in the milk, then liquidise.

Mix everything together in a bowl – the flakes of salmon, the potatoes, the liquidized garlic, the chives and the Tabasco. Adjust the seasoning and then – using 2 dessertspoons – mould the mixture into shapes that resemble miniature, plump canoes. Arrange 3 on a plate on top of the warm sauce in loose propeller formation.

FOR THE SAUCE

3 SHALLOTS, CHOPPED VERY FINELY	4 TABLESPOONS BALSAMIC VINEGAR
7 TABLESPOONS OLIVE OIL	SALT AND FRESHLY GROUND BLACK PEPPER

Mix all the ingredients in a saucepan, bring to the boil, and serve warm.

BABY SQUID WITH A BACON SAUCE AND PILAU RICE

9 SMALL SQUID	4 TABLESPOONS VEGETABLE OIL
3 SHALLOTS OR 1 MEDIUM ONION	1 SMALL GLASS PORT
4 SLICES SMOKED BACON	125ml (4fl oz) DOUBLE CREAM
1 GARLIC CLOVE	SALT AND FRESHLY GROUND BLACK PEPPER
1 SPRIG FRESH THYME	
1 BAY LEAF	

Clean the squid by cutting off the head, removing the innards and the transparent quill, washing, and then cutting into thin slices. Dry with kitchen paper.

To make the sauce, sweat the shallots in a pan with the bacon, garlic, thyme and bay leaf in half the vegetable oil for 10 minutes. Add the port and then the cream. Bring to the boil, season with salt and pepper and keep warm.

Finally, to cook the squid, heat a frying pan. When it's very hot, add the rest of the vegetable oil and the second it starts to smoke, throw in the squid and cook for 1 minute – and 1 minute only. Any longer and you end up with rubber.

Remove the squid from the pan, place on a warm serving dish and cover with the sauce. Serve with the pilau rice.

FOR THE RICE

1 SMALL ONION	125g (4oz) RICE
1 BAY LEAF	200g (7fl oz) WATER
1 SPRIG FRESH	SALT AND
THYME	FRESHLY GROUND
2 TABLESPOONS	BLACK PEPPER
VEGETABLE OIL	

Preheat the oven to 180°C/350°F/gas 4.

Sweat the onion, the bay leaf and the thyme in the oil with the rice – very gently – for 2 or 3 minutes. Add the water, season, bring to the boil, cover and finish off in the preheated oven for 10 minutes.

A Terrine of Orange, Grapefruit and Mint

For the Terrine

500ml (16fl oz)
ORANGE JUICE
SMALL BUNCH
OF MINT

12g (½oz) GELATINE
POWDER
4 ORANGES
4 GRAPEFRUIT

For the Light Chocolate Sauce

125g (4oz) DARK CHOCOLATE
125g (4fl oz) MILK

Heat the orange juice and steep the mint in it, as if making tea, until it has absorbed the flavour. Remove the mint. While the juice is still warm, add the gelatine.

With a small, very sharp knife, peel the oranges and grapefruit and cut out the segments, leaving behind the white fibre. Put the fruit into the terrine with half a dozen chopped mint leaves, and allow to set.

Serve with a very light chocolate sauce, made simply by warming the chocolate and milk together.

ALAIN PERDRIX
L'AVENTURE

Alain Perdrix is a delightful chef with a thin face, a baby daughter and a passion for food. Despite working with food all day long, he still enjoys talking about it. Time and again he'd describe a dish, and at the end pause and say: 'Ees bee-yoo-teeful.'

We first met in a wine bar in Holborn where his girlfriend used to work. There wasn't time for him to go home after lunch and get back in time to cook dinner in the restaurant, so he sat in a wine bar just down the road from the BBC World Service for a couple of hours every afternoon, drinking coffee and smoking. There's something very reassuring about pleasant people being in a certain place at a certain time, people you can drop in on. Like my My Friend the Travel Writer, sitting at home all day writing vivid tales of improbable journeys.

PARFAIT DE LÉGUMES
PROVENÇALES

1 RED PEPPER	A PINCH OF NUTMEG
1 GREEN PEPPER	4 TOMATOES,
A SMALL HANDFUL	SKINNED, SEEDED
OF GREEN BEANS	AND DICED
6 EGGS	VINAIGRETTE
SALT AND	
FRESHLY GROUND	
BLACK PEPPER	

Remove the skin from the peppers. The easiest way to do this is to put them under the grill and then straight into a tight bag for a minute or so. Then dice them.

Boil the beans until they're cooked *al dente*, then refresh them under cold water and dice them.

Preheat the oven to 160°C/325°F/gas 3. Beat the eggs, season with salt, pepper and nutmeg and add the peppers, beans and tomatoes. Divide the mixture equally between 6 buttered ramekin dishes and cover with foil. Place the dishes in a baking tray. Pour boiling water to half-way up the side of the dishes and cook slowly in the preheated oven for 40 minutes.

Meanwhile, make a mild vinaigrette. Use two thirds olive oil to one third vinegar; season with salt, pepper and a little mustard.

Add chopped shallot, chives and diced black olives to the vinaigrette, and pour a pool of vinaigrette on to each plate.

Ease the egg mixture away from the edge of the ramekin dishes and place in the centre of the vinaigrette.

POULET AU CITRON

1 CHICKEN
4 LEMONS
OIL FOR BRUSHING
THE CHICKEN
SALT AND
FRESHLY GROUND
BLACK PEPPER
1 TOMATO
200g (7oz) BUTTER

1 TABLESPOON
FRESH GREEN
HERBS, CHOPPED
(CHIVES, CHERVIL,
OR PARSLEY, OR A
MIXTURE – EVEN
MARJORAM, BASIL
AND CORIANDER
– IT'S LARGELY TO
ADD FRESHNESS AND
COLOUR)

FOR THE STOCK

1 CARROT
1 ONION
2 CLOVES GARLIC

1 STICK CELERY
1 BAY LEAF
6 PEPPERCORNS

Attack the chicken with a sharp knife, removing the 2 breasts from the carcass and both legs so you end up with 4 pieces of chicken. (For more than 4 people, you can slice the breasts in half lengthways and divide the legs at the joint just before serving. But leave them in 4 while cooking so they don't dry out.)

Put the carcass in 600ml (1 pint) of water with all the ingredients for the stock. Bring gently to the boil and simmer for an hour. Then strain, and reduce the stock to 150ml (¼ pint). The best way to do this is in a clean frying pan. It steams up the kitchen, but at least it doesn't take for ever. Otherwise just boil away in a saucepan to reduce it.

Remove the zest from one of the lemons with a sharp knife, making sure you don't get any pith. Then cut out the inner segments. It's a mildly fiddly process but not very difficult, as long your knife is sharp. Cut the top and bottom off the lemon so that it sits easily on the cutting board. Starting at the top, slice and saw downwards so that the skin and pith is removed, leaving the flesh of the lemon and the white whosits (membranes?) exposed. Then cut out each segment between the membranes. At the end, you should have half a dozen or so little segments of lemon flesh, and a flabby mass of white membranes which you throw away.

Slide the segments of lemon under the skin of the chicken, brush with oil, season with salt and pepper. Preheat the oven to 200°C/400°F/gas 6 and bang in the chicken. The breasts need around 15 minutes to cook, and the legs a little longer, around 20 minutes. They should be golden brown.

Meanwhile, make the lemon sauce.

Remove the zest and the juice from the remaining 3 lemons, adding the juice to the chicken stock.

Put the zest in cold water to cover, bring to the boil and then strain through a fine sieve. Repeat this process twice more to get rid of any hardness and bitterness in the zest.

Blanch the tomato in boiling water for a few seconds, then skin it, remove the seeds and dice the flesh into tiny cubes.

Divide the butter into small pieces and add it, piece by piece, to the stock over a low heat, stirring all the while. If you do it too fast or the heat is too high, the sauce will split.

At the last moment, just before serving, add the lemon zest, the chopped green herbs and the diced tomato. Pour the sauce over the chicken pieces and serve with boiled new potatoes and a very straightforward vegetable – courgettes or Brussels sprouts – bearing in mind that the sauce is very rich.

PETITE POIRE TATIN

5 PEARS, NOT   50g (2oz) BUTTER
TOO SOFT   200g (7oz) PUFF
150g (5oz) SUGAR   PASTRY

Preheat the oven to 200°C/400°F/gas 6.

Peel, core and quarter the pears.

Melt the sugar in the butter until brown rather than black. Watch it carefully, then add the pears and cook until brown and caramelised. Put into a round baking dish so that it fits flush – it doesn't have to be arranged prettily.

Roll out the pastry and cover the dish. The pastry will shrink, so make sure it goes over the edge. Bake in the preheated oven for 20 minutes until the pastry is brown.

Let it cool, and then refrigerate.

Putting a plate on top of the pastry, turn the whole thing upside down.

Note: If you have any difficulty turning it out, gently warm the base of the dish to soften the caramel to help it ease out.

Max Renzland
Le Petit Max

Max Renzland is one of these people who have the knack of making things work, so that even when bad things happen – which they frequently do – he's never going to be far away from jollity, excess and loadsamoney. He set up Le Petit Max with his identical twin brother Marc. Max did most of the front-of-house work, Marc was the chef.

Marc and Max. Max and Marc.

Le Petit Max is tucked under an embankment opposite Hampton Wick railway station. There's something indefinably magical about the place – the bare brick walls drip with contented karma. It's tiny. About eight tables covered in red-checked tablecloths. There's a square hole crudely cut through the wall separating the kitchen from the restaurant. And as for the decoration . . . Essentially, there is no decoration. And yet the place is infinitely welcoming. There's a feeling that nothing bad could happen there. When the winds blow and the hurricanes drench the steeples, we'll all be able to sit inside Le Petit Max in a cosy glow, count our blessings and know everything will somehow turn out all right in the end.

Max Renzland's father was German and his mother English. He and his brother were brought up in Essex. He looks like the lead singer in Alan Parker's *The Commitments*, plump rather than fat, with an extraordinarily young face and hair tied back in a ponytail. He has enormous energy. It's easy to imagine him leaping up and down on a dance floor, yodelling and pouring with sweat. He's vibrant and bright and bossy. Even in the middle of a conversation, he was aware of everything going on in the room. He'd suddenly stop what he was saying in midstream and start talking to the table next door, or else tell a waiter to bring more olives here or more coffee there. Everyone got the same cheerful, high-octane response from him – the customers, the waiters, the bloke who came to sort out the plumbing. And me. We all got it, one after the other. Sometimes all at once. If he'd had a mobile phone, it would have been ringing non-stop and every caller would have got it as well. He wheels and he deals and he chats and he fixes – he wasn't brought up in Essex for nothing. In the past, there may well have been a spot of bother with the VAT man along the way (there was) and a few taxes that might have gone astray (there were) and problems with bank managers and business partners (countless). There may even be a pair of white socks tucked away in a drawer somewhere. But the sheer, excessive fun of it all is contagious. Not so long ago, the Belgian mother of a friend bumped into the twins on a cross-channel ferry going to Calais, and described them as 'These amazing, extraordinary jolly chaps.' She'd never met anyone before like Marc and Max.

The food at Le Petit Max is rich, creamy, flavoursome bourgeois French cooking. Honest and generous. There's nothing the least ascetic about either Max or his food. It's possible to imagine him in a monastery, but it would have to be a pre-Reformation affair with a tolerant abbot, good ale and an abundant herb garden. In fact, platters of fresh food piled high on a long refectory table in front of a blazing fire with a Gregorian chant or two would probably suit him down to the ground. And no doubt many monasteries produced a wonderful goat's cheese *pour après*.

What is much more difficult is to imagine Max munching his way grimly through a plate of low-fat cottage cheese, a stick of celery and two slices of crispbread. Excess is the whole point. He'll talk about the numerous meals he's eaten at Le Gavroche and Tante Claire and the journeys he's made through France with Marc where they'd end up eating five meals a day. Not so long ago Max decided, for a change, to eat at home, so he cooked a meal for half a dozen friends and spent a cool £500 on sea-bass, caviare and wine. But the ultimate beneficiaries of that meal, of that excess, of that burning-of-candles-at-both-ends are the fortunate folk eating at Le Petit Max or the likes of me, who end up getting his very straightforward recipe for Toulouse sausages and haricot beans. The point is, Max is a man who loves his food. When he started to describe the menu, he turned into someone almost possessed. If that non-existent mobile phone had rung at that moment, who knows? He might even have ignored it.

Max and Marc served their apprenticeship together in Germany and Switzerland. They opened their first restaurant in Germany when they were twenty-one. They lived together and worked together most of their lives. Marc was inspired, obsessed, manic depressive – driven by every conceivable form of extremity and a few more besides. He didn't have a dull bone in his body. People who met Marc remember him, and the ones who ate his food vividly remember his cooking. But the one thing Marc wasn't big on, though, was moderation. A few months ago he died from a massive drug overdose, leaving Max to pick up a few thousand shards of broken glass.

He will, though. 'I'm going to be more Marc than Marc ever was,' he says. 'I'm going to out-Marc Marc.'

CREAM OF CELERIAC SOUP

700g (1½lb) CELERIAC
125g (4oz) UNSALTED BUTTER
A BOUQUET GARNI, TIED TOGETHER, CONSISTING OF: 1 CELERY STICK, CUT INTO 3, 3 SPRIGS FLAT PARSLEY, 1 SPRIG FRESH THYME AND 1 BAY LEAF

600ml (1 PINT) MILK
300ml (½ PINT) DOUBLE CREAM
SALT AND FRESHLY GROUND BLACK PEPPER
300ml (½ PINT) CHICKEN STOCK (OPTIONAL)
CHOPPED CHIVES

Peel the celeriac and chop into 2.5cm (1in) pieces.

Melt the butter in a saucepan and add the celeriac and bouquet garni. Cover and sweat for 5 minutes.

Add the milk and the cream. Bring to the boil and simmer until the celeriac is soft – about 8 minutes.

Remove from the heat, fish out the bonquet garni, liquidise and season. Add the chicken stock if necessary to prevent it being too thick, and serve with some freshly ground black pepper and a sprinkling of chives.

A DISH OF TOULOUSE SAUSAGES, HARICOT BEANS AND TOMATOES

500g (1lb) DRIED
HARICOT BEANS
100g (3½oz) DUCK
FAT, DRIPPING
OR LARD
6 LARGE TOULOUSE
SAUSAGES
1 LARGE ONION,
CHOPPED
100g (3½oz) BACON,
CHOPPED
A BOUQUET GARNI,
CONSISTING OF:
1 CELERY STICK,
CUT INTO
3, 3 PARSLEY STALKS,
1 SPRIG FRESH
THYME AND
1 BAY LEAF

4 WHOLE GARLIC
CLOVES
WATER OR CHICKEN
STOCK
2 LARGE CARROTS,
CUT IN HALF
LENGTHWAYS
400g (14oz)
TOMATOES, PEELED
AND SEEDED
SALT AND
FRESHLY GROUND
BLACK PEPPER
1 TABLESPOON
CHOPPED PARSLEY

Soak the beans overnight and drain them. Put them in a saucepan of water, bring it to the boil and simmer for half an hour. Drain.

Melt the fat in a large, heavy saucepan and fry the sausages until they're brown. Remove them from the pan.

Add the chopped onion and the bacon to the same pan and sauté for 5 minutes, then throw in the beans, the bouquet garni and the garlic with enough cold water or chicken stock to cover. Simmer gently, uncovered, for between 2½ and 3 hours, skimming off whatever scum rises to the surface. Add the carrots and the tomatoes after 1½ hours, and the sausages half an hour before serving.

The dish is ready when the water has reduced to just below the beans and become a thick sauce. Season and scatter with freshly chopped parsley.

CLASSIC CHOCOLATE CAKE MADE WITH VERY LITTLE FLOUR

I have a vague memory of a chocolate cake made with very little flour lurking in Elizabeth David somewhere. Max denies all knowledge of it. ('Who, me?') We'll just have to hope her estate aren't litigious.

275g (9oz) BITTER DARK CHOCOLATE	5 EGGS
275g (9oz) SUGAR	1 TABLESPOON FLOUR
165g (5½oz) BUTTER	ICING SUGAR

Preheat the oven to 180°C/350°F/gas 4.

Melt the chocolate, sugar and butter together in a bain-marie. Whisk the eggs and the flour together, and fold it into the chocolate mixture using a spatula.

Pour it into a cake tin that you've buttered and dusted with flour, then bake slowly in the preheated oven for between 35 and 40 minutes. It should still be fudgy in the middle.

When it's cool, dust with icing sugar and serve with cream.

GILBERT ROUSSET
MAGNO'S

Magno's is a French-style bistro in Covent Garden, with art-deco drawings and advertisements for Perrier water on the walls. There's a row of armagnac bottles lined up in front of the bar, the oldest dating back to 1918. Magno's caters to a lot of theatreland, and Gilbert Rousset looks like a younger version of Tom Stoppard.

Like so many other chefs I met, he was cheerful, pleasant and helpful. He laughed easily and obviously knew his oignons. It was nine o'clock, the morning after Easter. We sat down in the restaurant and drank coffee. I scribbled away in my notebook while he patiently took me through all the recipes. Remember, English is not his native language. He was doing it first thing in the morning, right after the holiday, when he had approximately three thousand other things to be getting on with. He was converting recipes designed for sixty people into quantities for six. He was having to explain processes that he does instinctively, turning them into specific directions. And it takes a lot of patience, if you're a chef, to stop in mid-sentence and explain to someone how much a knob of butter weighs. As if that wasn't enough, the recipes he gave me included pastry in the first course and gelatine in the dessert, which for me represents the quantum physics of cooking. But even having to explain all that didn't dampen his good cheer.

Afterwards, I asked him why he had come to England and where he had worked before. It transpired he had wanted a change from France. He went to an agency and they sent him off to Jersey. He loved the island. He married an English girl. They moved to London, and from 1985 to 1989 he worked at Magno's.

Then, in 1989, he set up his own restaurant. Unfortunately, it was in the wrong place at the wrong time. The bank manager was about to retire and was lending money to anyone who asked. There wasn't sufficient financial backing. Rousset worked sixteen hours a day. He never saw his family. And when the bank finally pulled the plug he lost his house. While he was telling me about it, the room got progressively darker, and by the time I left, he was heartily depressed.

Not much thanks for all his kindness.

FEUILLETÉ AU ROQUEFORT

25g (1oz) BUTTER	9oz (250g) PUFF
25g (1oz) PLAIN	PASTRY
FLOUR	1 TABLESPOON
300ml (½ PINT)	PARSLEY,
MILK	CHOPPED AND
150g (5oz)	1 TABLESPOON
ROQUEFORT OR	CHOPPED AND DICED
ANY STRONG BLUE	FLESH OF A TOMATO
CHEESE	FOR GARNISH (VERY
SALT AND	OPTIONAL)
FRESHLY GROUND	
BLACK PEPPER	
1 EGG	

FOR THE SAUCE

200ml (7fl oz) SINGLE CREAM
25g (1oz) ROQUEFORT

Melt the butter. Add the flour, stirring all the while to make a roux, and gradually stir in the milk. Then stir in the Roquefort until it has all amalgamated. Season with salt and pepper, remove from the heat and allow to get completely cold. It should have the texture of thick cream.

Next, separate the egg. Mix the yolk with a couple of tablespoons of water to make a wash (which you use later to brush the pastry) and keep the egg white to seal the edges of the pastry.

Roll out the pastry to a thickness of 3mm (⅛in), and divide into 6 oval shapes, each one about 20cm (8in) long.

Divide the cold Roquefort mixture into 6. Put a dollop on to one half of each piece of oval pastry. Then fold the other half of the pastry over, brushing the edges with egg white to act as a glue. Try to make the edges look as neat as possible – either use your thumb or a fork. Or – best of all – start at one end, and fold in little edges, one after the other, all the way round.

You end up with what looks like a cross between a very delicate Cornish pasty and the heel of a shoe, what les français call 'a slipper'. All this can be done way in advance and kept in the fridge.

Preheat the oven to 200°C/400°F/gas 6.

Brush the pastries with the egg-wash mixture, then put on a baking tray and bake in the preheated oven until golden brown. Serve immediately with the sauce.

FOR THE SAUCE

Bring the cream and the rest of the Roquefort to the boil. Reduce a little. Pour around each piece of pastry, and garnish with a little diced tomato flesh (remove skins and seeds) and the chopped parsley.

A CASSEROLE OF CHICKEN BREASTS WITH BASIL, YOGHURT AND TOMATO

300ml (½ PINT) CONCENTRATED CHICKEN STOCK	6 CHICKEN BREASTS
	2 SMALL (OR ONE BIG) TUB GREEK YOGHURT
25g (1oz) BUTTER	
25g (1oz) FLOUR	6 LEAVES OF BASIL
50ml (2fl oz) SINGLE CREAM	3 TOMATOES, SKINNED AND SEEDED
SALT AND FRESHLY GROUND BLACK PEPPER	50g (2oz) PEAS

First off, thicken the stock a little. Do this by heating the butter, stirring in the flour and whisking this roux mixture into the stock. Then add the single cream and correct the seasoning.

Next, put the chicken breasts, whole, under a hot grill or in a frying pan for 2 or 3 minutes just to seal them.

Then cut each breast into 5 or 6 pieces, add them to the sauce and cook for 15 minutes at the most.

Take the chicken out of the sauce and keep warm.

Then whisk in the yoghurt – don't, for heaven's sake, boil it in case it splits – and add the basil, tomatoes and peas. Return the chicken to the pan and heat through for a further 5 minutes, without boiling.

Pile it on to individual plates, a cascade of deliciousness, and serve with rice.

MOUSSE BRULÉE AU CARAMEL

75g (3oz) CASTER OR GRANULATED SUGAR
1½ LEAVES GELATINE (OR THE POWDERED EQUIVALENT)
4 EGG WHITES
75g (3oz) ICING SUGAR
150ml (5fl oz) SINGLE CREAM

First make a caramel by gently heating the caster or granulated sugar with ¾ tablespoon of water until it goes golden brown and is just beginning to smoke. Be careful, because it goes from brown to burnt very quickly. As soon as it's ready, stop it cooking by sticking the bottom of the pan into cold water.

Line a small terrine or plastic container – something about 12 cm (5in) long – with clingfilm.

Dissolve the gelatine into three-quarters of the caramel mixture while it is still warm.

Meanwhile, whisk the egg whites, and when they're almost stiff, add the icing sugar and continue whisking until they're very stiff. Fold in the caramel and gelatine mixture. Pour it into the terrine and put in the refrigerator to set. Divide into thick slices.

For the sauce, bring the cream and the rest of the caramel mixture to the boil, and then let it get cold. Pour over each slice of mousse.

Unarguably Italian

MADDALENA BONINO
BERTORELLI'S

Maddalena Bonino comes from an idyllic rural background in northern Italy. Her mother was from the south – 'a world of tomatoes, peppers, aubergines, squid, oil and chillies' – but she was born and brought up in the north. 'Full of risotto, polenta, mushrooms, veal, beef and butter. Much closer to French cooking.' She grew up commuting between two distinct cooking traditions. And while us lot in England were eating fish fingers and watching *Thunderbirds*, she was busy making jams and pickles, curing cheeses and bottling tomato sauces. By the time she was ten, she was able to bake bread and make pasta. Because both her parents worked, she did all the cooking for her three younger brothers, and from time to time helped out in a small restaurant run by family friends in the mountains of Piedmont.

She's lived in England for the past sixteen years. She came to learn the language, and found that speaking English was as effortless as cooking. She worked as an au pair and cooked for a family with five small boys. Robert Carrier ('Bob') used to drop by for meals, one of many people who kept telling her she should cook professionally.

And then, in the mid-1980s, she won the *Observer*'s Mouton Cadet Cookery competition. ('I did something very simple. Everyone else produced these fantastically complicated meals. All I did was a pasta with a dolcelatte sauce. And I didn't even make the pasta myself.') Now she cooks 500 meals a day at Bertorelli's. She's written a book on how to cook lovely food in less than half an hour. And she has a one-year-old son who laps up his pasta, his polenta and his couscous.

BRUSCETTA WITH MUSHROOMS

1 LOAF OF DAY-OLD
CIABATTA BREAD
3 TABLESPOONS
OLIVE OIL
25g (1oz) UNSALTED
BUTTER
2 GARLIC CLOVES,
ONE FINELY
CHOPPED, THE
OTHER CUT IN HALF
325g (11oz) BUTTON
MUSHROOMS,
THINLY SLICED

SALT AND
FRESHLY GROUND
BLACK PEPPER
450g (1lb) FRESH
SPINACH, WASHED,
DRAINED AND
ROUGHLY CHOPPED
1 LARGE TOMATO,
DICED
PARMESAN OR
CHEDDAR SHAVINGS

Cut the ciabatta in half horizontally and then cut each half into 3 pieces. Set aside ready to grill.

Heat the oil and butter in a large frying pan. When the butter starts to foam, add the chopped garlic and, immediately afterwards, the sliced mushrooms. Season with a little salt, and fry gently until the mushrooms are soft. Add the spinach, a little at a time, with the tomato, allowing each addition of spinach to wilt a little before adding the next lot. Check the seasoning and keep simmering lightly for a couple of minutes while you toast the bread.

When the ciabatta is ready, rub the cut side with the halved clove of garlic, arrange on individual plates, divide the spinach and mushroom mix equally between them and sprinkle with shavings of Parmesan or Cheddar.

SAUTÉ OF LAMB'S KIDNEYS WITH CANNELLINI BEANS AND A MUSTARD SAUCE

325g (11oz) WHITE
CANNELLINI BEANS,
SOAKED OVERNIGHT
3 TABLESPOONS
OLIVE OIL
50g (2oz) UNSALTED
BUTTER
18 LAMB'S KIDNEYS,
HALVED
1 MEDIUM ONION,
FINELY DICED

2 SPRIGS OF
FRESH THYME
2 TABLESPOONS
GRAINY MUSTARD
2 TABLESPOONS
BALSAMIC VINEGAR
½ WINEGLASS
WHITE WINE
SALT AND
FRESHLY GROUND
BLACK PEPPER

Cook the beans until soft and set aside.

In a large frying pan, heat 1 tablespoon olive oil with a small knob of butter. When the butter is on the point of burning, add the kidneys and fry quickly on both sides to sear and brown them. The fat for frying the kidneys needs to be very hot, so do the frying in 2 or 3 batches, removing the kidneys from the pan as they are ready, and keep warm.

Pour out any juices left in the pan and reserve them. Then return the pan to the heat with the remaining 2 tablespoons of oil. When it's hot, add the chopped onion and the thyme and gently fry until the onions are translucent and beginning to go crisp. Then add the cooked, drained beans.

Allow the beans to heat through before adding the mustard, vinegar, wine and seasoning. If you like your kidneys slightly pink, allow the beans to soak up the sauce by simmering for 10–15 minutes before returning the kidneys to the frying pan with any juices that you've kept. Otherwise, the kidneys can be added with the wine and vinegar and cooked in the sauce until ready.

Serve with boiled new potatoes or plain rice.

BAKED PEACHES WITH AMARETTI BISCUITS

3 LARGE OR 6 SMALL
PEACHES
6–8 AMARETTI
BISCUITS (OR
MACAROONS),
CRUMBLED

40g (1½oz)
UNSALTED BUTTER
1 TABLESPOON
ICING SUGAR
300ml (10fl oz)
DOUBLE CREAM

Preheat the oven to 240°C/450°F/gas 8.

Halve the peaches, remove the stones and hollow out each half with a teaspoon. Remove about 2 teaspoons of flesh from each half and mix it in a bowl with the crumbled biscuits, then return the mixture to each hollow.

Lightly grease an ovenproof dish big enough to lay all the peaches in, hollowed-out side up. Place a small knob of butter on each of the mounds of peach and amaretti mix, dust with half the icing sugar and bake in the preheated oven for 15 minutes for large peaches, 10 minutes for small ones. When they're ready, the top should be golden brown, and their own juices should be bubbling around the skins.

Remove from the oven and allow to cool for about 5 minutes, then dust with the remaining icing sugar and serve with double cream.

Vincenzo Borgonzolo
Al San Vincenzo

Vincenzo Borgonzolo – not a stage name – is the chef/proprietor of Al San Vincenzo in Connaught Street. It's a tiny family-run restaurant with a cult following, so dedicated to authentic Italian provincial cooking that it barely serves pasta. Even at the height of the recession, he had to turn people away every night. He sat in a tracksuit like an out-of-condition Italian footballer, smoking low-tar cigarettes, each one of which he rolled between his thumb and forefinger so that half the tobacco fell out before he lit it. ('What are you doing?' 'Getting rid of the tobacco,' he explained.)

As a child he preferred swimming in the Bay of Naples to sitting in a classroom. His mother consulted the local priest, who advised that he be sent away to boarding school – a cross between an orphanage and a reformatory. The food at the school was so deeply disgusting that his mother's cooking – with its emphasis on fresh ingredients and simplicity, the smell of garlic, olive oil and rosemary – wrought havoc with his subconscious.

He came to cooking very late. He started when he was forty and is entirely self-taught. Before that he was a bartender and his English wife a civil servant. Did he worry about opening a restaurant never having cooked professionally? 'Think positively! Always think positively! Think you're God! Behave like God! Then who will dare to question your talents?' His wife responds to any enthusiastic idea of his with an immediate 'Yes, dear,' only to wake up in the middle of the night three months later screaming with anxiety.

UOVA IN PURGATORIO (EGGS IN PURGATORY)

1 LARGE ONION, CHOPPED	SALT AND FRESHLY GROUND BLACK PEPPER
1 GARLIC CLOVE, CHOPPED	6 EGGS PER PERSON
OLIVE OIL	THYME (FRESH, IF POSSIBLE)
1 LARGE TIN (800g/ 28oz) TOMATOES	

Preheat the oven to 180°C/350°F/gas 4. Sweat the onions and the garlic in olive oil until soft but not brown. Using only the tomatoes, not the juice, squash the tomatoes with your hands into the onions and garlic (try to avoid splattering the walls), season with salt and pepper and cook for a few minutes.

Pour the tomato sauce into an oven dish. Carefully break the eggs on to the sauce with a scattering of thyme. Spoon some of the sauce over the top of the eggs, and bake in the preheated oven for 5 minutes, or until the eggs are cooked.

PIGEON CASSEROLE WITH LENTILS

6 PIGEONS	SALT AND FRESHLY GROUND BLACK PEPPER
OLIVE OIL	
2 LARGE ONIONS	450g (1lb) LENTILS
2 TURNIPS	ROSEMARY
2 POTATOES	1 BAY LEAF
4 CARROTS	
2 CELERY STALKS	

Cut 6 pigeons in half, sauté them in olive oil until they take on colour, and put them into a casserole. Sweat the vegetables in the olive oil with some seasoning, and add to the casserole.

Cook the lentils in water separately, but *not* until they're soft otherwise they'll become mush in the casserole. They should be harder than *al dente*, requiring a very definite bite. Drain them, reserving the liquid, and add them to the casserole.

Cover with the liquid from the lentils. Add rosemary and a bay leaf, season, and cook very gently in the oven on a low heat for 1½ hours. The texture of the casserole you end up with should be dense, neither dry nor wet, but creamy and fluid.

Serve with crusty bread.

CRESPELLE CON CREMA (PANCAKES WITH CUSTARD)

Pancakes are easy to make, hugely versatile, dirt cheap and loved by everyone. You can cook them in advance and pile them high on a plate in the oven. They're one of the most sociable of all kitchen activities: you can talk, drink and cook pancakes all at the same time. And they're the ultimate thing-to-do-with-your-hands for people giving up smoking.

The classic way to serve them is with lemon and sugar; jam is popular with children, but you can tart them up for a dinner party with a species of hot *crema pasticcera* and a sprinkling of grated chocolate.

FOR THE CRESPELLE

175g (6oz) FLOUR
2 EGGS
450ml (¾ PINT) MILK
A FEW KNOBS OF BUTTER

Put the flour in a mixing bowl and make a well in the middle. Break in the eggs, and gradually draw in the flour from the side of the well with a wooden spoon. When the mixture in the middle becomes too thick to absorb more flour, gradually add the milk. The batter should have the texture of sloppy mud. And if the worse comes to the worst and – heaven forbid – you end up with lumps ('Lumps, my dear duchess. *Lumps*') in your batter, put it through a sieve with the help of a wooden spoon. It's more washing up, but life's a bitch anyway. Leave to sit for half an hour.

The first pancake is the trickiest. Heat a knob of butter in a frying pan as hot as you can without it burning. Pour in some batter, tilting the frying pan this way and that so the batter spreads thinly and evenly. Leave on a medium heat for 2 or 3 minutes, then ease the crêpe away from the side of the pan and turn it over. There's no need to toss the pancake unless you're drunk. You'll find the other side of the pancake takes less time to cook.

FOR THE CREMA PASTICCERA

3 EGG YOLKS	25g (1oz)
75g (3oz) CASTER	CORNFLOUR
SUGAR	450ml (¾ PINT)
GRATED ZEST OF	MILK
1 LEMON	A SCATTERING OF
	GRATED CHOCOLATE

Cream the egg yolks, sugar and lemon zest together in the top of a double boiler or in a basin and gradually add the cornflour, dissolved in a little milk. Put the basin over a pan of boiling water, add the milk (which you've already warmed elsewhere to save time) and stir until it thickens.

A profoundly comforting, lemon-scented custard. Serve hot with the pancakes and sprinkle with grated chocolate.

Sandro Medda
OLIVO

No chefs look like chefs, but Sandro Medda looks even less of a chef than usual. He's young and dark and handsome and neat and earnest and a bit depressed. While he was thinking about the recipes, I tried to imagine what he would be if he wasn't a chef. A lawyer? A doctor? An architect?

Anyway. He was born in Sardinia and became interested in cooking while helping his mother. It prompted him to go to an Italian catering school, which was largely a waste of time because it was so old-fashioned. In retrospect, he reckons he would probably have been better off working in a half-way decent kitchen for a couple of years.

Then he went abroad. He spent two years in Geneva. Another year in Luxembourg, and in 1990 he came to England to learn English, and worked at the Hyde Park Hotel. The chef there, a man he liked enormously who left to open a restaurant in the US, taught him the importance of fresh ingredients and simple cooking, of putting things together in the right proportions. 'I discovered that you don't need to do difficult things to make them taste good.'

Medda was intending to go to Australia, but at his language school he fell in love with a Japanese girl and they got married. An Italian marrying a Japanese girl in London en route to Australia. They now have two children, a boy and a girl. He never did get to Australia. But just before he got married, he returned to Italy for six months to work at Gualtiero Marchesi's restaurant in Milan. Marchesi was a 'very nice, gentle person' who has 'without doubt' the finest restaurant in the whole of Italy, and manages to produce stunning results without using expensive ingredients. By using food, says Medda, 'correctly'.

As we got up to leave, he re-laid the table where we had been sitting. He very carefully put back the plates. He moved the glasses to where they had been before, smoothed the napkins and very precisely lined up the knives and forks. Then he checked the glasses to make sure they were at the right angle to the plates. It was like a Japanese tea ceremony in terms of its care and respectfulness. And then I realised what his manner reminded me of. Not a doctor or an architect, but a young priest.

CHILLED TOMATO SOUP

1.5kg (3¼lb) TOMATOES	A FEW DROPS OF BALSAMIC VINEGAR
SALT AND FRESHLY GROUND BLACK PEPPER	2 TABLESPOONS OLIVE OIL
	FRESH BASIL LEAVES

Get ripe, red tomatoes. Luscious, fat jobs with lots of flavour. Core them. Prick the ends and blanch them in boiling water for between 22 and 23 seconds. Then remove the skins and liquidise them with salt and pepper to taste. Add a few drops of balsamic vinegar to give the soup a little get-up-and-go, and then pass it through a sieve and refrigerate.

Stir in the olive oil, serve with some shredded basil on top, and don't be concerned or embarrassed by its simplicity.

PASTA ORECHIETTE WITH SUN-DRIED TOMATOES AND SALTED RICOTTA CHEESE

8 SUN-DRIED TOMATOES
100g (3½oz) SALTED RICOTTA CHEESE
1 SMALL FRESH RED CHILLI
450g (1lb) ORECHIETTE PASTA
2 TABLESPOONS OLIVE OIL
1 GARLIC CLOVE, CHOPPED
2 TABLESPOONS CHOPPED FRESH PARSLEY
SALT AND FRESHLY GROUND BLACK PEPPER

Chop the tomatoes and grate the cheese. Hold the red chilli pepper over a flame until it's blackened, then seed and chop it.

Boil and drain the pasta. Stir in the olive oil, the tomatoes, the garlic and the roast chilli, and sprinkle with grated cheese and chopped parsley. Season with salt and pepper.

SEMIFREDDO AMARETTI

2 EGGS
25g (1oz) CASTER SUGAR
3 DROPS OF VANILLA ESSENCE
150g (5oz) AMARETTI BISCUITS

Separate the egg yolks from the whites. Beat together the yolks and the sugar, add the vanilla, and stir in the crushed biscuits. Whip the egg whites firmly and fold them into the mixture. Then freeze it for between 4 and 5 hours. The texture is important. The mixture should be neither frozen rock-solid nor slopping all over the place. It should be *semifreddo* – somewhere between the two.

Sprinkle a crushed amaretti biscuit on each serving, and – if you can afford it – a dribble of amaretti liqueur.

Giancarlo Moeri
Como Lario

If you face the Royal Court Theatre, Como Lario is just down the road on your right. It's not an obvious choice for an impoverished gastronome – its specialities include dishes along the lines of smoked breast of duck with balsamic vinegar and cannelloni stuffed with seafood. In a previous restaurant, Giancarlo Moeri served hundreds of plates of spaghetti and lobster.

When I went to see him the first time, early on a Monday morning, both of his sous-chefs had fallen ill and he had been left to do everything on his own. Instead of pulling his hair out and telling me to take a running jump, he was very apologetic and immediately set about arranging another time.

'What about three o'clock on Friday?' he suggested.

But I had to be somewhere else later that afternoon.

'Two o'clock then?' he asked.

Usually any time between eleven o'clock in the morning and three o'clock in the afternoon is sacrosanct in kitchens, a time of maximum sweat, stress and clatter. But no, he said, two o'clock would be fine. And when I duly arrived at two o'clock on Friday, the place was in full swing – duck breasts and seafood cannelloni flying in all directions. He met me at the top of the stairs leading to the kitchen, ushered me to a private dining-room, and apologised once again for not being able to see me on Monday.

'But are you sure this is all right? Don't you need to be . . .?' I asked.

'No, it's fine,' he said. 'It's a great pleasure.' And as far as I could tell, he was completely sincere.

PENNE ORTOLANA

450g (1lb) PENNE PASTA	200g (7oz) UNSALTED BUTTER
1 TABLESPOON OLIVE OIL	3 TOMATOES, EACH QUARTERED LENGTHWAYS
1 GARLIC CLOVE, CHOPPED	1 SMALL SACHET SAFFRON POWDER
2 MEDIUM COURGETTES	½ HEAD OF RADICCHIO LETTUCE
1 HEAD OF BROCCOLI (125g/4oz)	1 BUNCH OF ROCKET
1 WINEGLASS WHITE WINE	

Cook the pasta in boiling salted water.

Gently heat the olive oil and garlic in a large frying pan for a minute. Then add the courgettes and the heads of broccoli with their stems – sliced and peeled – with the wine and the butter. Cook them gently for only about 2 minutes. When you bite into them, they should still have plenty of crunch.

Add the tomatoes, the saffron and the cooked pasta. Warm through, and at the very last moment – the second before serving – add the roughly chopped radicchio and rocket. Mix up everything, pile on to a plate and trickle with a little extra olive oil to give the dish a gloss finish.

Aside from being vegetarian heaven, this dish is monumentally colourful with the yellow, the red and the green.

PESCE ALLA GIANCARLO

6 GREY MULLET, OR THE EQUIVALENT	SALT AND FRESHLY GROUND BLACK PEPPER
4 SPRIGS OF THYME	6 WIDE SLICES OF SMOKED BACON
4 SPRIGS OF ROSEMARY	1 WINEGLASS WHITE WINE
4 SAGE LEAVES	300ml (½ PINT) CHICKEN STOCK
2 GARLIC CLOVES	
2 TABLESPOONS OLIVE OIL	

Clean the fish.

Preheat the oven to 180°C/350°F/gas 4. Chop together all the herbs and 1 clove of garlic. Mix them in a small bowl with the olive oil, salt and pepper. Stuff the fish with this mixture and then wrap bacon round each one.

Fry the fish very gently in olive oil with the rest of the garlic for 5 minutes on each side, then remove from the pan and transfer to an oven dish. Cover with the wine and chicken stock and bake in the preheated oven for 25 minutes.

Serve with boiled new potatoes and mangetout peas.

PEARS POACHED IN RED WINE

6 WILLIAM PEARS,	1 BOTTLE RED WINE
SLIGHTLY ON THE	3 TABLESPOONS
HARD SIDE	WHITE SUGAR
12 LEAVES OF	
FRESH MINT	

Peel the pears, but make sure you keep the stalks on. Place them carefully in a saucepan so that they can't move around.

Add half a dozen leaves of mint and the sugar, cover with red wine, and poach gently with the lid on for 12 minutes, more or less, after they've come to the boil. (You can always test them with a thin, skewer-like object.)

Cool and then chill the pears. To serve, put them on a large white dish, garnish each with a mint leaf and pour the syrup round.

Gino Santin
L'Incontro

Gino Santin is a busy and successful man, yet he was one of the few chefs who actually put pen to paper and answered my letter. What does this mean, I wonder? ('It means he's got a secretary,' said my wife.)

He wore expensive grey flannel trousers and an immaculately cut blazer. His hair was silver and perfectly manicured and his tummy discreet. Staff shimmered up to him and genuflected – could he please sign this? Could he please speak to so-and-so on the phone? But the joyous thing was his animation, the sparkle when he started talking about food. All the PR vanished, and here was simply a plump, enthusiastic, kindly, unpretentious Italian describing how wonderful food – even the cheapest food – can be.

Zuppa di Fagioli (Bean Soup)

350g (12oz) DRIED BORLOTTI BEANS	1 SCANT TABLESPOON CHOPPED PARSLEY
2 ONIONS, CHOPPED	OLIVE OIL
2 CARROTS, CHOPPED	1 HAM BONE OR SOME FRESH PORK
1 CELERY STALK, FINELY CHOPPED	SALT AND FRESHLY GROUND BLACK PEPPER
4 GARLIC CLOVES, CRUSHED	1 TABLESPOON PARMESAN CHEESE
1 SPRIG OF ROSEMARY	

Soak the beans overnight and drain. Sweat all the vegetables and herbs very gently in olive oil in a big saucepan for 5 minutes, then add the beans and stir for a couple of minutes to coat them.

Fill the pan with water, add the pork and simmer gently for approximately 2 hours. Exactly how long the beans take to cook will depend on their age. Towards the end of this process, add a healthy glass of olive oil. Remove one third of the beans, and put the rest through the food processor with the meat (obviously removed from any bones). Return to the pot with the whole beans, check for seasoning, simmer for 5 minutes, then let the soup stand for 10 minutes. Trickle a little olive oil in each bowl of soup with a sprinkling of Parmesan cheese, and serve with crusty bread.

RISOTTO D'ORTICHE (RISOTTO OF STINGING NETTLES)

A risotto is a very wonderful thing, but there are a couple of things to remember. You must be prepared to spend half an hour, non-stop, stirring it on the stove, adding the stock a little at a time. If you want to wander around passing the peanuts, forget it. And a risotto, a proper risotto, should always have a gooey, creamy consistency.

1 ONION, CHOPPED	350g (12oz)
2 WHOLE GARLIC	ARBORIO RICE
CLOVES	1.2 LITRES
OLIVE OIL	(2 PINTS) STRONG
450g (1lb) STINGING	CHICKEN STOCK
NETTLES (WEAR	A KNOB OF BUTTER
RUBBER GLOVES,	FRESHLY GRATED
AND USE THE	PARMESAN CHEESE
TENDER TOPS),	1 TABLESPOON
CHOPPED	CHOPPED PARSLEY

Gently sauté the onion and garlic cloves in olive oil for a few minutes. Stir. Remove the garlic and add the chopped nettles. Stir. Add the rice. Stir. Add 3 ladles of hot stock. Stir. It will start to become creamy – don't add so little stock that the risotto dries out, or so much stock that the rice boils. Creaminess is all. Add 2 more ladles of stock. Stir. And keep doing this, adding stock a little at a time and stirring until all the stock is absorbed and the rice is cooked. The rice should retain a slight bite, *al dente* rather than mush. Stir in the butter, Parmesan and parsley.

A note on chicken stock: Try to avoid cubes. They give everything a nasty chemical aftertaste. Just get a chicken carcass from your friendly neighbourhood butcher or a few chicken wings and simmer them with pretty much whatever you've got to hand. (Within reason, obviously. Best not to throw in the rhubarb, the cup cakes or the glacé cherries.) Onions, garlic, bay leaf, carrots, leek, winter vegetables, parsley, celery, thyme, etc. etc. It's not at all a bad idea to refrigerate the stock overnight, dump the hardened fat and reduce the stock by a third.

POLENTA PASTICCIATA

The 'Polentoni' were those too poor to buy bread. Polenta pasticciata is simply a lasagna – with fewer layers – made with polenta instead of pasta. But polenta is something well worth writing home about, and so cheap it used to be fed to the pigs.

FOR THE POLENTA

1.2 LITRES (2 PINTS) WATER	2 TABLESPOONS FRESHLY GRATED
1 TABLESPOON SALT	PARMESAN CHEESE
250g (9oz) POLENTA	CHOPPED PARSLEY

Heat the water to simmering and add the salt. Gradually trickle the polenta into the water a little at a time, stirring all the while until it is all absorbed and you've got a yellow porridge that gets thicker as you go along. Continue stirring for half an hour – by which time your arm will ache and you'll be telling yourself it's just not worth the effort. Press into a cake tin. When it's cold, it'll become a hefty sponge which you can then slice into lasagna-like leaves.

FOR THE TOMATO SAUCE

Quite rightly, everybody has their own recipe for tomato sauce – and I make no claims that this is The Way to Make a Tomato Sauce or even that it's an especially good one. There's a perfectly sound recipe for tomato sauce in *The Godfather Part 1* in the scene just before Sonny is murdered. For what it's worth, this is the one I use:

1 LARGE ONION, CHOPPED	A WINEGLASS RED WINE IF YOU'VE GOT IT
2 GARLIC CLOVES, CHOPPED	1 HEAPED TABLESPOON EACH
OLIVE OIL	CHOPPED CELERY
450g (1lb) MINCED LAMB OR BEEF	AND PARSLEY
1 LARGE TIN (800g/28oz) TOMATOES	WHATEVER HERBS YOU'VE GOT: MARJORAM, BASIL, THYME, ROSEMARY
1 HEALTHY TEASPOON SUGAR	LEAF
	SALT AND PEPPER

Sauté the onion and garlic in olive oil in a frying pan and brown the mince. Pour off any excess fat, add all the other ingredients and cook slowly for an hour or so. Season to taste.

FOR THE BÉCHAMEL SAUCE

50g (2oz) BUTTER	SALT AND
50g (2oz) FLOUR	FRESHLY GROUND
600ml (1 PINT) MILK	BLACK PEPPER

Melt the butter, add the flour and stir. Add the milk, a little at a time, stirring all the while. If lumps develop, don't panic, just whisk. It should end up creamy and lump-free. Season.

71

Preheat the oven to 160°C/325°F/gas 3. Butter a dish and cover the base with thinly sliced polenta. Spread a layer of tomato sauce, then a layer of béchamel, then another layer of polenta, a layer of tomato sauce, and so on. Onwards and upwards. Sprinkle the Parmesan over the top. Bake in the preheated oven for an hour or so until the cheese is golden, then scatter with chopped parsley.

TIRAMISU

6 EGG YOLKS	36 SPONGE FINGERS
SUGAR TO TASTE	600ml (1 PINT)
500ml (16fl oz)	STRONG BLACK
DOUBLE CREAM OR	COFFEE, COOLED
MASCARPONE	UNSWEETENED
A DASH OF WHISKY,	COCOA POWDER
BRANDY OR RUM	

Beat the egg yolks with a little sugar and mix into the cream or mascarpone. Add a generous dash of alcohol and beat until fluffy.

Soak the sponge fingers briefly in the coffee and use half to line the bottom of a serving dish. Arrange half the whipped cream carefully on top, then another layer of soaked sponge fingers. Cover with the rest of the cream and dust the top lightly with cocoa. Refrigerate until needed, or serve immediately.

AURELIO SPAGNUOLO
DEL BUONGUSTAIO AND OSTERIA ANTICA BOLOGNA

If someone asked me which was my favourite recipe in the book, polpette di poveri – meatballs without meat – would be on the short list. It couldn't be easier, and it just goes to show how many roads lead to Rome. If you want to learn to cook, you can slave away for years in a subterranean French kitchen, go to an expensive cooking school, or sit up all night reading recipes from Sri Lanka and Normandy, Tunisia and Mexico and experiment on your friends. You can buy Delia Smith. Alternatively, you can do what Aurelio Spagnuolo did, which is to make sure that you're born into a large family in a small village outside Bologna where you and your brother do most of the cooking and fourteen people regularly sit down to a meal. That way, sooner or later, you'll end up producing something as good and cheap and simple as polpette di poveri.

He now has two restaurants, Del Buongustaio and Osteria Antica Bologna, both of which reflect his firm belief in authentic regional Italian cooking – food as eaten in Italian homes. Del Buongustaio, just the other side of the Thames on the Putney Bridge Road, has no carpet. The walls are essentially bare. Each table has a candle. There are a couple of rotating fans in the ceiling. The afternoon I went, a very appreciative baby was being fed in the corner – a baby being given a head start in life.

POLPETTE DI POVERI (POOR MAN'S MEATBALLS)

FOR THE POLPETTE

450g (1lb) BREADCRUMBS	2 EGGS
6 GARLIC CLOVES	A LITTLE WATER (TO BIND THE MIXTURE)
SMALL BUNCH OF FRESH MINT	SALT AND FRESHLY GROUND BLACK PEPPER
3 TABLESPOONS GRATED PARMESAN CHEESE	VEGETABLE OIL FOR FRYING
1 TABLESPOON PINE-NUTS	

Finely chop the polpette ingredients as necessary and mix them all together except for the oil. Shape to the size of golf balls – 3 or 4 per person – and then slightly flatten them so that they end up looking like miniature ice-hockey pucks.

Heat the oil, fry them for 5 minutes or so on each side until they're golden brown, and arrange them on a plate on top of the raw tomato sauce.

FOR THE RAW TOMATO SAUCE

6 RIPE RED TOMATOES	1 TABLESPOON OR SO OLIVE OIL
SALT AND FRESHLY GROUND BLACK PEPPER	A FEW DROPS OF RED WINE VINEGAR
A FEW LEAVES OF FRESH BASIL	1 GARLIC CLOVE

Cut the tomatoes in half and then grate them with the cut side of the tomato facing the grater. That way, you end up left with the skin of the tomato in your hand, which you can then just throw away.

74

Season the pulp with the salt, pepper, basil, olive oil, vinegar and garlic.

PENNE AL TOSCO (PASTA WITH ROSEMARY, GARLIC AND CHILLIES IN A TOMATO SAUCE)

450g (1lb) PENNE
PASTA (APPARENTLY
DE CECCO PASTA, IN
A BLUE PACKET, IS
THE BEST AVAILABLE
IN ENGLAND)
6 GARLIC CLOVES,
CHOPPED

3 TABLESPOONS
FRESH ROSEMARY
LEAVES
5 GREEN CHILLIES,
SEEDED
3 TABLESPOONS
OLIVE OIL

FOR THE TOMATO SAUCE

1 ONION, FINELY
CHOPPED
4 GARLIC CLOVES
CHOPPED
1 TABLESPOON
OLIVE OIL
1 BIG TIN (800g/
28oz) CHOPPED
TOMATOES

½ TEASPOON SUGAR
A FEW LEAVES
OF BASIL
SALT AND
FRESHLY GROUND
BLACK PEPPER

First make the tomato sauce. Sweat the onions and the garlic in a little olive oil in a saucepan; add the tomatoes, sugar, basil, salt and pepper and cook for 20 minutes only. Cook it for longer and you end up with a tomato concentrate flavour, which is not something you want.

Put the pasta to cook in a large pan of boiling water. While it is cooking, chop the garlic, rosemary and chillies very finely and heat, very gently, in the olive oil for a couple of minutes. As soon as it starts to smell, add the tomato sauce and cook for a further 5 minutes to amalgamate all the flavours.

To serve, mix half the mixture into the cooked pasta with the other half on top. Only put grated Parmesan on top if you're desperate to – the flavour will overpower the rosemary and the chillies.

POLPETTE DI RICOTTA

This recipe dates from ancient Rome, although in those days they used honey instead of sugar.

250g (9oz) RICOTTA
1 EGG
100g (3½oz) FINE
BREADCRUMBS
100g (3½oz)
GROUND ALMONDS
1 TABLESPOON
CASTER SUGAR
VEGETABLE OIL FOR
FRYING
4 TABLESPOONS
WARMED HONEY
FRESHLY GROUND
BLACK PEPPER

Mix the ricotta, egg, breadcrumbs, almonds and sugar together and shape into slightly flattened golf-balls.

Heat the oil and fry the golf-balls until they're golden on both sides. Put them on a plate, cover with the honey and grind black pepper on top.

EAST OF SUEZ

Mrs Atalla
Al Bustan

Al Bustan is a Lebanese restaurant in Belgravia, full of potted plants and pale green trelliswork. There weren't any peacocks strutting their stuff or delicate fountains tinkling away, but there easily could have been. It was that sort of place.

Mrs Atalla – who runs the kitchen with a fierce energy – has been in England for almost twenty years. Her marriage was arranged when she was seventeen. 'My husband was working in England as a hotel manager. Every year he returned to Jerusalem on holiday. I suppose he must have finally got fed up with being nagged by his family to get married. He was a decent, likeable man from a good family and besides, I was the third of three daughters. I didn't want to get married. I did it to please my father. Within a week we were engaged and two months later we were married.' She paused. 'From Jerusalem to London in the middle of February. The buildings were all so dull. The people so unfriendly. It was hard.'

When I spoke to her on the phone she said she was very busy, what with a restaurant to run and three children. She could only see me for half an hour, she said. So I met her on Sunday evening, stopwatch at the ready. Small cups of fiendishly strong coffee were brought. Then a plate of tiny baclava. Then glasses of tea. Then more glasses of tea. Two and a half hours later we'd covered the failings of the various food guides, the Middle Eastern peace initiative, the correct way to chop parsley, life in Gerrards Cross, the Oxford entrance exam and racism among the British police. And she gave me a recipe for a lamb and spinach stew with coriander and lemon that I dreamt about that night.

HOUMOS

450g (1lb)	2–3 ICE CUBES
CHICKPEAS, SOAKED	JUICE OF 2 LEMONS
OVERNIGHT AND	SALT AND
RINSED THREE TIMES	FRESHLY GROUND
1 TEASPOON	BLACK PEPPER
BICARBONATE	CUMIN, PAPRIKA
OF SODA	AND CHOPPED
5 TABLESPOONS	PARSLEY TO GARNISH
TAHINI	OLIVE OIL

Simmer the chickpeas with the bicarbonate of soda until soft. Drain and process in a blender, then add the tahini and the ice cubes to help it get the right texture. Finally, add the lemon juice and season to taste. Sprinkle with paprika and cumin, garnish with chopped parsley and a dribble of olive oil, and serve with hot pitta bread.

TABBOULEH

75g (3oz) BURGHUL	4 TABLESPOONS
4 BUNCHES FLAT	OLIVE OIL
PARSLEY	A PINCH OF
6 TOMATOES	DRIED MINT
1 BUNCH OF SPRING	SALT
ONIONS	1 COS LETTUCE, TO
JUICE OF 3 LEMONS	GARNISH

Pour boiling water over the burghul to cover. Cut the stalks off the parsley (roughly half-way). Retain the stalks for the Bakdonesieh salad. Roll and turn the bunches of parsley into crude ropes, and chop them very finely. Cut them only once: don't chop over them or mince them. Chop the tomatoes and the spring onions. Mix together the parsley, burghul, spring onions, tomatoes, lemon juice, olive oil and salt. Arrange in the centre of a dish surrounded by the lettuce, which you use to scoop up the tabbouleh.

BAKDONESIEH

PARSLEY STALKS FROM THE TABBOULEH (ABOVE)	2 TABLESPOONS TAHINI
1 GARLIC CLOVE	JUICE OF 3 LEMONS
½ HOT GREEN CHILLI, SEEDED	SALT

Chop the parsley stalks very finely and mix with all the other ingredients.

LAMB, SPINACH AND CORIANDER STEW (SABANECK)

1.8kg (4lb) SHOULDER OF LAMB	1 BUNCH OF CORIANDER
2 TABLESPOONS OLIVE OIL	JUICE OF 2 LEMONS
1 BAY LEAF	SALT AND
6 GARLIC CLOVES, FINELY CHOPPED	FRESHLY GROUND
1.4kg (3lb) SPINACH, WASHED WELL AND DRAINED	BLACK PEPPER

Bone the lamb, remove the fat and cut into cubes. Brown the meat in olive oil in a frying pan, then cover with water and simmer for at least an hour with the bay leaf until the meat is tender and the liquor reduced to 300 ml (½ pint).

Sweat the garlic gently in a little oil, then add the spinach and coriander and cook for 3 minutes. Add the meat and the stock, cook for 10 minutes more, then season and add lemon juice to taste.

Serve with plain white rice.

MUHALABIYEH

1.2 LITRES (2 PINTS) MILK
125g (4oz) SUGAR
1 TABLESPOON ROSEWATER OR ORANGE BLOSSOM WATER

1½ TABLESPOONS CORNFLOUR, DISSOLVED IN A LITTLE WATER
A HANDFUL OF CHOPPED NUTS AND SULTANAS TO GARNISH

Bring the milk and the sugar to the boil with the rosewater or orange blossom water. When it's boiled, add the cornflour, stirring all the time. Remove from heat, put in a dish and decorate with chopped nuts and sultanas.

Serve with cold kater, a syrup made from two parts of sugar to one part of water simmered for half an hour on a gentle heat and allowed to cool.

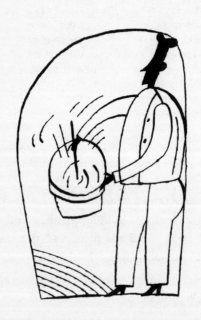

FRANCES AND ABDEL BOUKRAA
ADAM'S CAFÉ

Adam's Café is at the Dorset end of Shepherd's Bush, off the A40. If you're coming from central London, you go through Knightsbridge, head past the Brompton Oratory on your right, then straight down that awful Cromwell Road and round a number of roundabouts, making sure you get off at the right exits. That's important. Otherwise you end up doing what I did, which is going round in circles. It's a question of getting into the right lane at the right time, which is difficult to do on a bicycle in the pouring rain in very heavy traffic when you've gone from one end of London to the other and you're soaked to the skin and completely bloody lost. You end up wobbling indecisively round roundabouts. Lorry drivers hoot at you. And you panic. Wobble – hoot – panic. Life in a nutshell. And really all one needed was someone to say: 'Listen, cretin. Head straight for Shepherd's Bush – ask any taxi driver to direct you. Then it's a mile or so down the road from there.' But the trouble is, My Friend the Travel Writer, who's very good at that sort of thing, suddenly had a rush of blood to the head and moved to Inverness to write a book on Burma, so I can hardly ring him up at peak time and ask him what the A40 means in English. As a result, I arrived at Adam's Café very late and very wet.

Adam's Café specialises in Tunisian food. No surprise, since Abdel is Tunisian. Frances, on the other hand, is English, the Marianne Faithful of the couscous world. When they applied for a loan from the bank, they arrived in the manager's office laden down with cash-flow charts and sharpened pencils, business plans and pocket calculators. The manager was suitably impressed. He asked them what sort of food they were going to serve.

'Couscous.'

'Ah,' he said. 'I see. Couscous.' There was a slight pause. Then he asked: 'What exactly *is* couscous?'

'Well, it's . . . it's semolina.' They didn't get the loan.

So Adam's Café never gave up its day job. From nine to five it is still gainfully employed serving eggs and bacon and paying its taxes. But at night, as the sun sets on Acton, you're invited to 'reserver votre table' in order to 'deguster nos specialités'. And then the place starts teeming with Cambridge graduates in their late twenties tucking into couscous.

TUNISIAN SALAD

1 CUCUMBER	1 MEDIUM ONION
3 MEDIUM TOMATOES, SEEDED BUT NOT PEELED	2 HARD-BOILED EGGS
	12 BLACK OLIVES
1 GREEN PEPPER	1 TABLESPOON
1 SMALL APPLE	TINNED TUNA, TO GARNISH (OPTIONAL)

FOR THE DRESSING

OLIVE OIL	SALT AND
JUICE OF 1 LEMON	FRESHLY GROUND
1 TEASPOON	BLACK PEPPER
DRIED MINT	

Dice the vegetables and apple into tiny pieces the size of confetti.

Mix them all together, pour on the dressing, and garnish with the eggs cut into wedges, the olives and the tuna. (This is not a tuna salad, so if you're tempted to use a whole tin, best leave it out altogether.)

FISH COUSCOUS

3 MEDIUM ONIONS
3 BIG POTATOES
2 GARLIC CLOVES
6 CARROTS
6 COURGETTES
6 SMALL SWEDES
1.4kg (3lb) GREY
   MULLET
2 TABLESPOONS
   CORN OIL OR
   OLIVE OIL
2 SMALL TINS
TOMATO PURÉE

¼ TEASPOON
POWDERED SAFFRON
½ TEASPOON
   GROUND
   CORIANDER
1 TEASPOON
   GROUND CUMIN
   HARISSA SAUCE
   TO TASTE
1 TIN CHICKPEAS
900g (2lb) COUSCOUS

(Harissa sauce is murderously hot. So you're on your own as to how much you want to put in. Less is probably more, because masochists can always add more at the table.)

To cook the stew:
Roughly chop the vegetables.

Scale and gut the fish, and cut into thick 5cm (2in) steaks. The important thing is to keep the fish in healthy chunks to stop it falling apart during the cooking.

Sweat the onions, garlic and potatoes in the oil. Add the tomato purée, the spices and the harissa sauce, mix, and cover with 1.7 litres (3 pints) of water. Bring to the boil, then add all the vegetables, except for the courgettes which take less time to cook.

Simmer for 20 minutes, or until the vegetables are half cooked.

Add the fish, the chickpeas and the courgettes to the stew, and cook for another 15 minutes. The vegetables should be cooked through but still firm, and the fish should not be falling to pieces.

To cook the couscous:

Either follow the directions on the supermarket packet, which is something I've always done and it seems to work fine, or put the couscous into a fine-meshed sieve and let it sit in cold salted water for 30 seconds before lifting it out to drain. It will have absorbed enough water. Then steam it for 15 minutes, timing it from the moment the steam starts appearing through the couscous – which means that it's heated through. (You can use one of those Chinese bamboo steamers. Or sit it on top of a saucepan of boiling water in the fine-meshed sieve. Or, best of all, use a proper couscoussier if you happen to be one of the fortunate four people in England who owns one. With a couscoussier, the couscous sits on top of the stew while it cooks, absorbing all the flavours.)

After 15 minutes, tip it out, fluff up the grains between your fingers, and then put it back into the steamer to heat through once more.

Probably the easiest way to serve it is to have one bowl for the couscous, another for vegetables (with a ladle for the sauce) and a separate plate for the fish. With the harissa sauce as a dangerous little dish on the side.

MINT TEA

1.2 LITRES (2 PINTS) WATER	SMALL BUNCH OF FRESH MINT
2 TEASPOONS GREEN (GUNPOWDER) TEA	1 TABLESPOON SUGAR

Boil the water in a saucepan. Add the tea, the mint and the sugar. Let it steep for a couple of minutes, then bring back to the boil, strain and serve in glasses. If you have oranges and branch dates to go with it, so much the better.

Hemant Desai
Sabras

Sabras is in Willesden, of all places. Willesden. Beyond Neasden. ('I didn't think you were going to see restaurants outside London,' said My Friend the Travel Writer.) Getting to Willesden from Tottenham involved another kamikaze bicycle ride, along the North Circular. One significant gust of wind, one wobble of the wheels and you'd be not merely dead but unrecognisable. Parachutists, I'm told, never entirely lose the fear of jumping, and they can always tell you the precise number of jumps they've made. I feel exactly the same way about the North Circular.

Sabras is not merely in Willesden, but it's been there for the past twenty years. It's a small, very inexpensive, squeaky-clean Indian vegetarian restaurant opposite the Brent Women's Centre and the Venus Fish Bar. It's conveniently situated a couple of doors away from an Afro barber shop and a solicitor's office, who 'assist in very urgent overnight domestic violence – matrimonial. *Injunctions* and similar injunctions like land/tenancy dispute.'

On the walls are a wide assortment of award certificates and newspaper cuttings heaping praise on Sabras, alongside a Polaroid snapshot of Ken Livingstone eating a bhajee.

BANANA PAKODA, WITH APPLE AND ONION CHUTNEY, AND A YOGHURT SAUCE

6 BANANAS
OIL FOR DEEP-FRYING

FOR THE BATTER

200g (7oz) GROUND
BESAN FLOUR (MADE
FROM CHICKPEAS)
3 HOT GREEN
CHILLIES
2.5cm (1in) FRESH
GINGER, PEELED

1 TABLESPOON
CHOPPED
CORIANDER
PINCH OF TURMERIC
JUICE OF 1 LEMON
SALT
WATER

For the batter, blend all the ingredients together, adding sufficient water to give the batter the consistency of thick double cream. Slice the bananas into thick coins, dip them in the batter, and deep-fry them in oil until golden brown.

APPLE AND ONION CHUTNEY

1 LARGE ONION
1 COOKING APPLE,
PEELED AND CORED
3 TEASPOONS SUGAR
1 TEASPOON SALT

½ TEASPOON CHILLI
POWDER
½ TEASPOON CUMIN
POWDER

Shred the onion and the apple and mix all the ingredients. That's it, folks. But this is so good you might consider doubling the quantities and making twice as much.

YOGHURT SAUCE

2 CUPS PLAIN NATURAL YOGHURT	½ TABLESPOON CHOPPED CORIANDER
½ TEASPOON SALT	
½ TEASPOON SUGAR	

Mix.

POPPADUMS

Heat in advance over a gas flame with a pair of tongs. Rub with butter, fold in half and in half again – like a crêpe – before they have time to stiffen.

BOMBAY POTATOES

450g (1lb) POTATOES	3 TABLESPOONS OIL
2 ONIONS	1 TEASPOON CUMIN SEEDS
1 GARLIC CLOVE	1 TEASPOON MUSTARD SEEDS
50g (2oz) PEANUTS	2 TABLESPOONS TOMATO PURÉE
2 TEASPOONS GARAM MASALA	1 TABLESPOON CHOPPED FRESH CORIANDER
½ TEASPOON TURMERIC	
2 TEASPOONS DESICCATED COCONUT	

Peel and boil the potatoes, and slice them while still hot – this prevents the potatoes becoming sticky.

Put the onions, garlic, peanuts, garam masala, turmeric and coconut into a blender and make a paste, adding a little water if necessary.

Heat the oil in a frying pan and add the cumin and mustard seeds. As soon as they start to crackle, lower the heat and add the paste from the blender, cooking for 10 minutes on a low heat. Then add the potatoes, tomato purée and water to cover, and simmer for a further 5–10 minutes on a very low heat. Finally, add the chopped coriander. Serve with rice.

THE RICE

450g (1lb) BASMATI
RICE
WATER (SEE BELOW)
JUICE OF 1 LEMON
125g (4oz) FROZEN
PEAS

SALT
½ TEASPOON CUMIN
½ TEASPOON
TURMERIC
A KNOB OF BUTTER

Put the rice in a measuring jug and measure out three times its volume in water. Wash the rice twice. Bring the water to the boil. Add the rice and the lemon juice. Cook for 20 minutes, drain and allow to cool.

Meanwhile, steam the peas. Toss them in the salt, cumin and turmeric and add to the rice. Cover and heat through very gently with a knob of butter.

SHIRO (SEMOLINA HALVA)

50g (2oz) UNSALTED
BUTTER
150g (5oz) SEMOLINA
900ml (1½
PINTS) MILK
100g (3½oz) SUGAR

1 TEASPOON
GROUND
CARDAMOM
25g (1oz) RAISINS OR
SULTANAS
25g (1oz) CASHEWS

Heat the butter, add the semolina and cook on a low heat for 10 minutes, stirring continuously. Add the milk, sugar, cardamom, raisins and cashews. Stir, then cover and simmer for 10–15 minutes on a low heat. It should be firm rather than liquid. Serve warm.

Laurent Farrugia
Laurent's

Couscous summons up images of scorching midday sun, of heat so strong the lizards look for shade. A world of whitewashed walls, teeming markets, brightly coloured cotton robes, mint tea and hashish. On the other hand, some of the best couscous in England is to be had at Laurent's on the Finchley road in NW2, turning left off the North Circular by a derelict Vauxhall showroom.

Laurent Farrugia – the chef/proprietor – looks like a suspicious cherub. 'I don't give my recipes to nobody,' he said, with his arms folded in front in him. Could he perhaps suggest a meal – a couscous for half a dozen people – that wouldn't result in the immediate closure of his restaurant? 'What can I tell you?' he asked with an exasperated shrug. 'Couscous is a stew. So you cook a stew.' But Mr Farrugia, please. Couscous is very cheap. It would be perfect for people who are greedy and broke. You're the finest couscous chef in London. Couldn't you . . .?

LAURENT'S RELUCTANT COUSCOUS

1 LARGE ONION, CHOPPED
1.4kg (3lb) NECK OF LAMB
2 TABLESPOONS OLIVE OIL
2.4 LITRES (4 PINTS) WATER
1 LARGE TABLESPOON TOMATO PURÉE
2 STICKS CINNAMON
4 GARLIC CLOVES
1 TEASPOON TURMERIC
450g (1lb) CARROTS, CHOPPED
½ SMALL HEAD OF CELERY, SLICED
2 TURNIPS, CHOPPED
½ SHREDDED WHITE CABBAGE
1 TIN CHICKPEAS
4 TABLESPOONS CHOPPED FRESH CORIANDER
4 TABLESPOONS CHOPPED PARSLEY
SALT AND FRESHLY GROUND BLACK PEPPER
450g (1lb) COUSCOUS

Sweat the onions and brown the meat in olive oil in a casserole dish. Add the water, the tomato purée, the cinnamon sticks, the garlic and the turmeric, and cook gently until the meat is tender. A couple of hours. When the meat is almost ready, add the carrots, celery, turnips, white cabbage, chickpeas, coriander and parsley. Season to taste.

Put the couscous into a bowl, cover with boiling water, and steam in a muslin-lined colander for about 15 minutes.

Serve the stew and the couscous in separate bowls, accompanied by harissa (red chilli) sauce.

FOR THE HARISSA

125g (4oz) DRIED
HOT CHILLIS
(SOAKED IN WATER
AND DRAINED)
6 CLOVES GARLIC
4 TABLESPOONS
COARSE SALT

6 TABLESPOONS
CORIANDER SEEDS
4 TABLESPOONS
CUMIN SEEDS
8–10 TABLESPOONS
VEGETABLE OIL

All of which you pulverise together in a pestle and mortar, gradually adding the oil. Dangerous, dangerous stuff.

(I asked Laurent what you'd start off with. 'Couscous is big meal. You don't need a starter,' he said. Or a dessert? 'Whatever you like. Mint tea. Baclava. You know baclava? Whatever you like.')

YOUSIF MUKHAYER
THE MANDOLA

If Saddam Hussein was a few years younger and spent his life being pleasant to people rather than killing them, he'd look a bit like Yousif Mukhayer. His Sudanese restaurant, the Mandola in Westbourne Grove, has five tables covered in red oilcloths, and you bring your own drink. There's a gas heater on wheels if it's a chilly night. The walls are pale green and yellow. The kitchen is at one end, with the salads laid out on show in front – aubergines marinating in oil; a mound of shredded rocket leaves and crumbled feta; a bowl of smooth tahina next to a white cabbage salad with peanut and lime dressing.

Yousif Mukhayer is the self-appointed cultural ambassador for the Sudan, but the Sudan he represents is not the unsmiling country of Islamic fundamentalism and military dictatorship. It's a Sudan where the coffee is spiced with cloves, cardamom, cinnamon and ginger. A country of cold-pressed sesame oil and red hot chillies, of pulses and cumin and coriander, a world bursting with sunshine and hospitality. As I bicycled home from his restaurant that night, I barely noticed a gale that was blowing down trees and fences all over London.

FOUL (PRONOUNCED 'FOOL')

Traditional Sudanese cooking doesn't involve the starter and main course of Western cooking – the food is served all at once. This is essentially a one-course meal, which you eat with large quantities of hot pitta bread. All you'll need after it is some fresh fruit.

1kg (2¼lb) DRIED BEANS, SOAKED OVERNIGHT	6 TOMATOES
	1 BUNCH ROCKET LEAVES
2 ONIONS	175g (6oz) FETA CHEESE
GROUND CUMIN	
SALT	1 TABLESPOON CHILLI SAUCE
3 TABLESPOONS OLIVE OIL	

FOR THE FALAFEL

450g (1lb) DRIED CHICKPEAS, SOAKED OVERNIGHT IN COLD WATER	2 HOT GREEN CHILLIES
	1 TEASPOON BAKING POWDER
3–4 GARLIC CLOVES	SALT
1 BUNCH OF SPRING ONIONS	VEGETABLE OIL FOR FRYING
3 TABLESPOONS EACH CHOPPED DILL, CORIANDER AND PARSLEY	

To make the falafel, first cook the soaked chickpeas till tender, drain them, and process them with the garlic, spring onions, dill, chillies, coriander and parsley. (Spring onions and dill are the basis – the addition of other herbs is glorious luxury.) Add the baking powder and salt to taste, and roll into golf-balls. Heat the oil until it's just beginning to smoke, then turn the temperature down and deep-fry the falafel for 7 minutes or so until they're golden brown and cooked.

Meanwhile, cook the beans in boiling water until soft – roughly 3 hours. Add the chopped onions for 5 minutes just before the beans are cooked.

Drain the beans and season with cumin, salt and oil to taste. Put them in a dish and scatter on the chopped tomatoes and the rocket leaves, then the falafel – roughly crumbled – then the grated feta, more cumin and the chilli sauce.

95

TOMATO SALAD

6 TOMATOES

FOR THE DRESSING

JUICE OF 3 LIMES
1 SMALL JAR
SMOOTH PEANUT
BUTTER
1 BUNCH OF SPRING
ONIONS, CHOPPED

1 TABLESPOON
COLD-PRESSED
SESAME OIL, OR
OLIVE OIL
3 GREEN CHILLIES
SALT AND GROUND
CUMIN TO TASTE

Chop the tomatoes. Mix the rest of the ingredients to make the dressing and combine with the tomatoes just before serving – if you do this too soon the tomato liquid will all drain out.

THE BEDLINGTON CAFÉ

T ell someone with a car to head down the A4 towards Heathrow and get off in the labyrinth of suburbia around Chiswick, they wouldn't bat an eyelid. But doing it on a bicycle from north London is a different matter – with juggernauts howling past you every twenty seconds you feel like a jogger in the middle of a Grand Prix. Then of course I managed to get completely lost, and you can't stop and ask directions on the A4. Still, I got there. Eventually.

Quite apart from the fact that the Bedlington Café serves very superior and inexpensive Thai food, it isn't a café at all. But that's to be expected – after all, the Museum Street Café isn't a café either. But whereas the Museum Street Café is more of a bistro, the Bedlington Café is a caff, a very definite two-f caff with absolutely nothing é about it. Not even the most fanciful romantic could talk up its charms, with its formica tables, pale blue plastic chairs, linoleum floor and filthy ceiling, all glaringly picked out in bright fluorescent light. A person could eat there every single day without compromising their extreme Trotskyist revolutionary principles.

Mrs Priyanu is a large and tired lady, and she treated me with weary acceptance. Whenever she lost interest while explaining the recipes to me – which was quite frequently – the man who washes the dishes would prompt her. 'Make sure the meat is finely chopped,' he'd say. On the inside of the door is a sign that says, 'Welcome to the Bedlington Café. Please enjoy your meal' (underlined), while another notice asks you to use the ashtrays provided.

It's a very odd place. While I was there, a man phoned to book a table the following night – from Oslo.

97

DEEP-FRIED PRAWN TOASTS WITH SWEET AND SOUR RELISH

125g (4oz) MINCED
PORK
6 LARGE PRAWNS OR
20 SMALL ONES
1 TABLESPOON
SOY SAUCE
1 SPRING ONION,
CHOPPED

SALT AND
FRESHLY GROUND
BLACK PEPPER
4 PIECES OF BREAD
OIL FOR
DEEP-FRYING

FOR THE RELISH

2 TABLESPOONS
SUGAR
1 TEASPOON SALT
3 TABLESPOONS
VINEGAR

2 TABLESPOONS
WATER
1 SMALL CARROT
2.5cm (1in) PIECE OF
CUCUMBER
¼ SMALL ONION

Mash the pork and the prawns with the soy sauce and the chopped spring onion. Season, spread on the bread, and deep-fry until golden brown. Drain on kitchen paper. Cut each slice of bread into 4 triangles and arrange on a plate with the relish in the centre.

For the relish, first dissolve the sugar and salt in the vinegar and water. Allow to cool. Finely dice the vegetables and add to the liquid just before serving.

The main course consists of three meat dishes – pork, beef and chicken – a vegetable dish and a bowl of rice. All the work is in the preparation, so settle down with a very sharp knife and a radio play.

STIR-FRIED BEEF WITH CHILLIES, ONIONS AND GARLIC

480g (1lb) BEEF
(TOPSIDE)
3 HOT GREEN
CHILLIES, DE-SEEDED
1 SMALL ONION
2 SPRING ONIONS

1 GARLIC CLOVE
2 TABLESPOONS
VEGETABLE OIL FOR
FRYING
1 TABLESPOON
SOY SAUCE

Slice the beef into thin 2.5 cm (1in) ribbons. Cut the chillies, onion and spring onions lengthways into thin 2.5 cm (1in) strips. Chop the garlic.

Heat the oil and stir-fry the beef for 3 minutes with the onion, garlic and soy sauce on a high heat. When the beef is nearly cooked, add the chillies and stir for a few seconds, and finally add the spring onions for another 5 seconds or so.

Keep in a warm place until ready to serve.

SIAMESE PORK

450g (1lb) PORK
1 GARLIC CLOVE
1 SPRING ONION
2 TABLESPOONS
VEGETABLE OIL FOR
FRYING
1 TABLESPOON
SOY SAUCE

½ TEASPOON SALT
FRESHLY GROUND
BLACK PEPPER
2 TABLESPOONS
WATER
1 TABLESPOON
FINELY CHOPPED
FRESH CORIANDER

Cut the pork into 1cm (½in) cubes. Chop the garlic. Cut the spring onion lengthways into 2.5cm (1in) pieces.

Heat the oil and stir-fry the pork with the garlic over a high heat for 5 minutes or so until the pork is cooked. Add the soy sauce, salt, pepper and the water. Finally, throw in the finely chopped coriander and the spring onions and stir for a further 15 seconds.

Keep warm, until ready to serve.

STIR-FRIED CHICKEN WITH GINGER

250g (8oz) BONED CHICKEN	2 TABLESPOONS VEGETABLE OIL FOR FRYING
½ ONION	
4cm (1½in) FRESH GINGER	2 TABLESPOONS SOY SAUCE
1 SPRING ONION	A PINCH OF SALT
1 SMALL RED PEPPER	1 TABLESPOON WATER

Cut the chicken into very thin strips. Chop the onion. Peel the ginger. Slice it thinly, lengthways, and do the same for the spring onion and the red pepper.

Heat the oil. Stir-fry the chicken and onion for 2 minutes, then add the soy sauce, the ginger, the pepper, salt and water.

Keep warm until ready to serve.

STIR-FRIED MIXED VEGETABLES

1 GARLIC CLOVE	2 TABLESPOONS VEGETABLE OIL FOR FRYING
2 HEADS OF BROCCOLI	
½ SMALL CAULIFLOWER	1 TABLESPOON SOY SAUCE
3 CARROTS	A PINCH OF SALT

Chop the garlic. Use the small flowerets of the broccoli and the cauliflower. Dice the carrots into thickish matchsticks.

Heat the oil and add the garlic, making sure it doesn't burn. Add the vegetables and stir fry with the soy sauce and the salt for 1½ minutes on a high heat.

BANANAS IN COCONUT MILK

200ml (7fl oz)   2 TABLESPOONS
COCONUT MILK   SUGAR
200ml (7fl oz) WATER   1 TEASPOON SALT
    6 BANANAS

Bring all the ingredients to the boil in a saucepan, except for the bananas.

Meanwhile, cut the bananas in half lengthways and then into 7.5cm (3in) slices. Add them to the saucepan, return to the boil and serve immediately.

PRETTY POSH

Tom Benham
MONKEYS

Tom Benham looks like Santa Claus. He went to Marlborough and later worked as a chartered accountant with substantial periods in between misspending his youth. He was a bit vague about the precise details of the misspending, but it didn't involve being detained by Her Majesty (I asked). Having never trained or cooked professionally, he took over the kitchen when the chef at Monkeys left.

He sat me down and gave me the best meal I've eaten for as long as I can remember. A bed of salad with warm fillet of salmon to start off with, the salmon moist and melting. Then a mound of scallops, quartered and sautéd to the colour of roast potatoes, the flesh inside succulent, and surrounded by the freshest and greenest of green beans. Oh dear, oh dear, it was good. And then a slice of lemon tart to end up with. Lemon tart? Lemon tart. If anyone ever thinks lemon tart sounds dull, try this one.

LEEK TERRINE WITH A VINAIGRETTE

1.8kg (4lb) TRIMMED LEEKS	SALT AND FRESHLY GROUND
125g (4oz) COOKED LENTILS	BLACK PEPPER
	VINAIGRETTE

Wash the leeks (cut along each one lengthways with a knife to within a couple of centimetres – an inch – of the root and wave it around in water so it spreads out like a flower and any dirt washes away.) Trim to the length of the terrine. Simmer in water until *al dente*.

Line a terrine with clingfilm so there's a healthy overlap. Using a pair of rubber gloves, put the leeks in the terrine while they're still hot, seasoning each layer. Alternate the layers to make it more attractive, so that one layer has the root-end facing one way, the next layer has them facing the other way. Every third layer, put a layer of cooked lentils.

Keep piling on layers until it's 4 or 5 inches above the top of the terrine. Fold the clingfilm over on two sides, then put another terrine on top – or a bit of wood cut to size – and put on top of this some very, very heavy weights. Put it in a bowl or a sink, because a great deal of water is going to come off.

Every hour or so, pour off the water and refold the clingfilm. Eventually the leeks will have compressed to the height of the terrine. Leave overnight, still weighted down, and slice carefully.

Serve with a vinaigrette.

STUFFED BREAST OF LAMB

2 BREASTS OF LAMB (1.4kg/3lb)	1 TABLESPOON TOMATO PURÉE
VEGETABLES:	½ ONION
CARROT/CELERY/ ONION/LEEK/GARLIC	1 CUP BREADCRUMBS A BUNCH OF SAGE
1 BAY LEAF	1 EGG
SALT	

The day before, put the lamb in a large casserole, cover with water and any vegetables you have lying around – carrot, celery, onion, leek, garlic – a teaspoon of salt, a bay leaf, and the tomato purée. Simmer very, very gently so the water is barely turning, for at least 4 hours. You'll be able to remove any fat or bones effortlessly. Strain, and allow the stock to cool. Then refrigerate and simply take off the fat, and reduce the stock to 300ml (½ pint) for gravy. You can add any winter vegetables to cook in the reduced stock like a pot–au–feu to serve with the lamb

Preheat the oven to 190°C/375°F/gas 5.

Chop the onion and add to the breadcrumbs with the chopped sage. Bind with an egg and spread on top of one breast. Put the other breast on top like a sandwich, force into a rounded sausage shape, and tie with string in the middle and at each end. Cook in the preheated oven for 20 minutes or so.

LEMON TART

125g (4oz) BUTTER	100g (3½oz)
275g (9oz)	CASTER SUGAR
PLAIN FLOUR	4 EGGS
125g (4oz)	150ml (5fl oz)
ICING SUGAR	DOUBLE CREAM
ZEST AND JUICE OF 2	
LEMONS	

Make a pastry by rubbing the butter, flour, icing sugar and chopped rind of one lemon together until crumbly, then add 1 egg, beaten, and roll into a ball. Let it rest in the fridge for an hour.

Preheat the oven to 180°C/350°F/gas 4.

Roll out the pastry and put it into a flan tin. Bake blind (cover with a layer of greaseproof paper and a pile of dried beans) for 15 minutes. Remove the beans and paper and bake for another 15 minutes.

For the filling, whisk the remaining 3 eggs, the caster sugar and remaining lemon zest. Fold in the cream and lemon juice. Pour into the base and bake for half an hour. It's ready when it's reasonably firm – the middle should be slightly underdone because it'll go on cooking after it's been taken out. If you let it cook too long, the filling will shrink when it cools and leave an unsightly chasm between the outer edge of the pastry and the filling.

FULHAM ROAD, STEPHEN BULL'S BISTRO, STEPHEN BULL AT BLANDFORD STREET

The way I did this book was to write to various chefs first and then ring them up a couple of days later. Sometimes they were too busy. Other times – not very often – they just didn't want to get involved.

One of the very first chefs I rang up has a restaurant in south London. The voice that answered the phone was cheerful and breezy, but as soon as I told him who I was, it switched from friendly to ice cold. 'Yes,' he said, 'I did get your letter.' There was silence the other end of the line. I asked if it might be possible to come down and talk to him. 'No, you can't,' he said, and banged down the phone.

Later that day – a *lot* later that day – I gathered up what few tattered shreds of courage I had left and rang up another chef, Stephen Bull, who comes heavily armed with a reputation for being one of the people responsible for the enormous improvement in English food over the past ten or fifteen years. Without a moment's hesitation he said he'd see me. I was so surprised I vaguely remember blurting out something like, 'Are you *sure*?' Yes, he said, he'd be very pleased to help.

So far as I'm concerned, Stephen Bull walks on water. May all his restaurants flourish. May his house be free of tigers. May his baby daughter grow up to be kind, creative, thoughtful and beautiful and look after him in his old age.

108

JERUSALEM ARTICHOKE SALAD

700g (1½lb) JERUSALEM ARTICHOKES	4 TABLESPOONS SUNFLOWER OIL
3 SHALLOTS OR 2 RED ONIONS, FINELY CHOPPED	3 TABLESPOONS RED OR WHITE WINE VINEGAR
2 TABLESPOONS CHOPPED PARSLEY	1 TEASPOON DIJON MUSTARD
GRATED RIND OF 1 LEMON	SALT AND FRESHLY GROUND BLACK PEPPER
3 TABLESPOONS OLIVE OIL	

Scrub the artichokes and cut into 1cm (½in) slices. Boil in salted water for 10 minutes, then drain and refresh under cold water.

Make a vinaigrette with the rest of the ingredients and dress the artichokes, preferably a couple of hours before serving.

FILLET OF PORK WITH ANCHOVIES AND BASIL

1 SMALL PORK
FILLET, OR
TENDERLOIN
(400g/14oz)
1 SMALL TIN
ANCHOVY FILLETS
12 BASIL LEAVES
(OPTIONAL)
25g (1oz) GRATED
PARMESAN CHEESE

1 EGG
1 TABLESPOON MILK
50g (2oz) PLAIN
FLOUR
BUTTER FOR FRYING
SALT AND
FRESHLY GROUND
BLACK PEPPER

Trim the pork of any excess fat and membrane.

Slice the pork into 12 medallions, and using a heavy knife, a wooden mallet, a rolling pin or a milk bottle, flatten out each slice as flat as possible.

Divide the anchovies into 12 equal portions, and place them on each piece of pork with a basil leaf on top. Strictly speaking, you can do without the basil. 'It's a bit of a luxury,' quoth Mr Bull, 'and it works perfectly well without it.' Then sprinkle on some salt and pepper, fold each piece of pork over – the end bits may look a bit misshapen, but never mind about that – and press the edges firmly together. This much can be done in advance.

Then mix the cheese, egg and milk in one bowl, and put the flour in another.

Dip each piece of pork into the egg wash and thence into the flour so that it's well coated.

Heat 15g (½oz) of butter in a frying pan, and fry the pork in batches for 3 minutes each side. Replenish the butter as needed and keep the cooked pork warm on a hot serving dish.

Serve with pasta and small Brussels sprouts or broccoli.

PEANUT BUTTER CHEESECAKE

50g (2oz) BUTTER	150g (5oz) SMOOTH
8 DIGESTIVE BISCUITS	PEANUT BUTTER
225g (8oz) CREAM	½ TEASPOON
CHEESE	VANILLA ESSENCE
125g (4oz)	150ml (5fl oz)
ICING SUGAR	WHIPPING CREAM

Melt the butter, crush the biscuits and mix the two. Press the mixture evenly into a 15cm (6 in) springform or loose-bottomed cake tin. A larger tin will do, but obviously the cheesecake won't be so high.

Cream the cheese well, add the sugar and peanut butter and cream again until the mixture lightens considerably. Use a wooden spoon or a food processor. Add the vanilla essence and fold in the half-whipped cream.

Transfer to the cake tin and smooth the top. Refrigerate for several hours. Run a knife between the cheesecake and the tin, and remove to a large plate.

111

192

Working at 192 in Notting Hill doesn't automatically guarantee fame and fortune, but it's a bit like winning the New Hampshire primary – it helps.

Take Adam Robinson and Maddalena Bonino. They both worked there. Both are wonderful cooks and so pleasant they deserve to be on the receiving end of every last passing gust of half-way decent karma floating around central London.

Then there's Alastair Little. He used to work there. *Everyone* knows of Alastair Little. My eighty-plus aunt-in-law who lives on top of a hill in Greece with a large cat has heard of him. Angela Dwyer worked there. Josh Hampton. And now Albert Clarke. If the cooking world is like the Chancery Bar, a small community where everyone knows everyone else, 192 is a distinguished set of chambers.

Albert Clarke first learned to cook at the Groucho Club when he was sixteen before moving to 192. Then off he went to Los Angeles and worked in kitchens over there. He didn't bother with niceties like a green card – 'It was all strictly on the fiddle.' He was forced to return to London after a couple of years when he lost his driving licence for repeated speeding and couldn't get around Los Angeles without a car.

He became head chef at a restaurant called Wilds, which closed down after he left. From there, he ran the kitchens at the Halycon Hotel, every moment of which he loathed. There was something infinitely dispiriting about cooking for rock stars who'd eat nothing but wholewheat pasta at four in the morning. Besides, he hated the whole business of working in a hotel: 'It's like being on stage twenty-four hours a day.'

Before he returned to 192 as head chef, he set up his own company dedicated to producing ice-cream, in commercial quantities, without additives, preservatives, flavouring or any other petroleum-based products. Proper ice cream, in other words. And he's still only twenty-six.

ROASTED TOMATO SOUP WITH CHILLI CRÈME FRAÎCHE

1.5kg (3¼lb) PLUM TOMATOES

1 TABLESPOON VEGETABLE OIL

SALT AND FRESHLY GROUND BLACH PEPPER

5 GARLIC CLOVES

1 CARROT, DICED

1 LEEK, DICED

1 ONION, DICED

1 CELERY STALK, DICED

1 ORDINARY RED CAPSICUM PEPPER, SEEDED AND DICED

1 CHIPOTLE CHILLI (SEE BELOW)

1 TEASPOON TOMATO PURÉE

1 TEASPOON WHITE SUGAR

ZEST OF ½ LEMON

A FEW SPRIGS OF FRESH CORIANDER

BOUQUET GARNI

2 TABLESPOONS OLIVE OIL

7.5cm (3in) OR SO OF THE SKIN-END OF A BIT OF PARMESAN CHEESE (THIS NEED NOT HAVE CHEESE ON IT – JUST THE END BIT THAT YOU'D NORMALLY THROW AWAY)

600ml (1 PINT) CHICKEN STOCK

FOR THE CHILLI CRÈME FRAÎCHE

1 RED CHILLI (PLUMB, 7.5cm (3in) LONG, USUALLY FROM KENYA AND AVAILABLE AT ANY SUPERMARKET)	1 SMALL TUB OF CRÈME FRAÎCHE JUICE OF ½ LEMON FRESH CORIANDER LEAVES FOR GARNISHING

Turn on the oven as hot as it will go. Put the tomatoes in a roasting dish with the vegetable oil, seasoned with salt and pepper, along with 2 whole garlic cloves. Roast them in the oven until they blacken and begin to break up. This will take between 30 and 40 minutes.

Meanwhile, dice the carrot, the rest of the garlic, the leek, onion, celery and pepper, and sweat for 20 minutes. Then add the chopped chipotle chilli, the roasted tomatoes, tomato purée, sugar, lemon zest, coriander stalks (keep the leaves for garnishing), along with some salt and pepper, the olive oil and the end piece of Parmesan. Add the chicken stock and simmer for 20 minutes on a low heat.

Blitz in a liquidiser and strain. Serve with a dollop of chilli crème fraîche.

For the chilli crème fraîche: roast and blacken the chilli, either in a hot oven or over a gas ring with a pair of tongs. Skin, seed and chop it. Mix it into the crème fraîche with the lemon juice, and garnish with coriander leaves.

Note: The chipotle is a smoked jalapeño chilli with a smoky, nutty flavour. Available from the Cool Chilli Co. (tel. 01973 311714). Unfortunately, it is essential you use this pepper.

CHICKEN AND FENNEL RISOT

2 HEADS FENNEL
1 WHOLE HEAD
OF GARLIC, CUT
IN HALF (FOR
THE STOCK) AND
1 EXTRA GARLIC
CLOVE FOR THE
RISOTTO ITSELF
1 CARROT,
ROUGHLY CHOPPED
1 LEEK, ROUGHLY
CHOPPED
1 CELERY STALK,
ROUGHLY CHOPPED

FRESH OR DRIED
THYME
2 BAY LEAVES
6 CHICKEN LEGS
150g (5oz) BUTTER
1 ONION, DICED
100g (3½oz)
ARBORIO RICE
75g (3oz) GRATED
PARMESAN
1 SMALL BUNCH
PARSLEY, FINELY
CHOPPED

FOR THE ROCKET SALAD

225g (8oz)
ROCKET LEAVES,
WASHED, WITH A
STRAIGHTFORWARD,
NO-PONCING-
AROUND DRESSING
MADE WITH:

3 TABLESPOONS
OLIVE OIL
JUICE OF 1 LEMON
SALT AND
FRESHLY GROUND
BLACK PEPPER

Trim the fennel by cutting off the tops and bottoms – you use those bits for the stock. Keep the frizzy dill-like leaves for garnishing right at the end. Finely dice the main body of the fennel, and set aside to put in the risotto.

Then put all the vegetables and herbs – everything except for 1 bay leaf, the onion and the diced fennel – into a litre (1¾ pints) of water with the chicken legs. Bring to the boil and simmer gently for half an hour.

Remove the chicken legs from the broth, and when they've had time to cool a little, take the flesh off the bone and put on one

115

side. Strain the broth and reduce it by half. All this can be done in advance.

When it comes to making the risotto itself, melt 100g (3½oz) of butter in a frying pan and sweat the diced onion and fennel with the extra chopped garlic clove and the second bay leaf. When the onion and garlic have softened, add the rice and stir until all the grains are well coated.

Stirring gently the whole time with a wooden spoon, making sure no grains of rice get stuck to the side of the pan, slowly add the hot chicken broth, half a ladle at a time, until the stock is absorbed and the rice is cooked. Finally, when the rice is cooked, stir in the rest of the butter to give it a glossy coating, then add the grated Parmesan, the finely chopped parsley and the frizzy bits of fennel, chopped up.

Check the seasoning and serve with the rocket salad.

BLOOD ORANGE GRANITA

225g (8oz) SUGAR	600ml (1 PINT)
600ml (1 PINT)	FRESH ORANGE
WATER	JUICE, MADE FROM
ZEST OF 2 ORANGES	ROUGHLY 14 BLOOD
	ORANGES
	JUICE OF 2 LEMONS

Boil the sugar and water with the zest of the 2 oranges. Once the sugar has melted, let it cool.

Add the juice of the blood oranges and the lemons. Then put in a plastic container in the freezer for 8 hours or so, stirring every hour. It should have a texture somewhere between crunchy ice and slush, 'like a sorbet gone wrong. It's very refreshing – it cuts through all the fat of the meal.'

MARK HIX AND TIM HUGHES
LE CAPRICE

It's true what the *Good Food Guide* said – they're nice to you at Le Caprice, even if you aren't rich or famous.

Mark Hix is the thirty-two-year-old executive head chef of Le Caprice and the Ivy, who looks like a failed contestant from an Elvis Presley lookalike contest – all blue suede shoes and immense charm. He produced these recipes at nine o'clock in the morning off the top of his head, while simultaneously answering the telephone, ordering boxes of chanterelles from a visiting rep and tasting wild boar sausage. 'Naaa . . . Needs more mincing. Too lumpy. That's the trouble with wild boar – it can be tough. The taste's there, though. Could do with a bit of braising, maybe? Dunno. We'll see.'

CREAMED ONION AND CIDER SOUP

350g (12oz) SLICED ONIONS	1 WINEGLASS CIDER
50g (2oz) BUTTER	900 ml (1½ PINTS) VEGETABLE STOCK
1 BAY LEAF	1 SMALL CARTON CREAM
1 SPRIG OF FRESH THYME	SALT AND FRESHLY GROUND BLACK PEPPER
1 TABLESPOON FLOUR	

Sweat the onions in the butter slowly in a saucepan, without colouring. Cover and continue cooking slowly with the bay leaf and the thyme for another 10 minutes, until the onions are soft.

Add the flour and continue to cook for a minute or so, then stir in the cider. Gradually add the vegetable stock, whisking to

avoid lumps. Bring slowly to the boil and simmer gently for
1½-2 hours.

Right at the end add a little more cider and the cream, and
correct the seasoning.

CONFIT DE POULET

6 FAT CHICKEN LEGS AND WINGS	1 TEASPOON TOMATO PURÉE
SALT AND FRESHLY GROUND BLACK PEPPER	4 CARROTS
2 GARLIC CLOVES	2 CHICKEN STOCK CUBES
25g (1oz) FLOUR	175g (6oz) STREAKY BACON
1 LARGE ONION	1 SMALL SAVOY CABBAGE
FRESH OR DRIED THYME	CHOPPED PARSLEY
1 BAY LEAF	

First attack the chicken by separating the legs from the wings.
Reserve the wings. Chop off the short end-bit of the leg at the
knuckle and remove the thigh bone, so what you're left with is the
drumstick minus the thigh bone. Reserve the trimmings. Season the
legs with salt, pepper and one of the cloves of garlic, crushed. Dust
with flour, and cook in a very low oven (160°C/325°F/gas 3) for
1½ hours. If there's sufficient fat, baste from time to time: the meat
will become tender, the skin very crisp.

Meanwhile, make the stock. Roughly chop half the onion and
brown it with the wings and trimmings. Add the garlic, thyme,
bayleaf, tomato purée, carrots and stock cubes and pour on 900
ml (1½ pints) of water. Bring to the boil, skim, and simmer for
an hour – then put through a fine sieve and reduce to a mere 150
ml (¼ pint).

Dice the other ½ onion very finely, chop the bacon into 1cm
(½in) pieces and cook in a large frying pan over a low heat until

soft. Chop the cabbage roughly into 2.5cm (1in) squares, and add to the pan. Season with salt and pepper, and cook over a low heat, stirring constantly, for 30 minutes.

Turn the oven very high, and put in the chicken legs for a 3-minute blast of heat to crisp them. Lay the legs on a bed of cabbage, pour round the sauce and scatter with the parsley. Serve with sautéd garlic potatoes.

SAUTÉD GARLIC POTATOES

900g (2lb) NEW
POTATOES
3 TABLESPOONS
OLIVE OIL
2 GARLIC CLOVES

SALT AND
FRESHLY GROUND
BLACK PEPPER
1 TABLESPOON
CHOPPED PARSLEY

Parboil the potatoes, cut them in half, and sauté them gently in the olive oil and garlic. Season and scatter with parsley.

CREAMED RICE AND APRICOT BRULÉE

50g (2oz) PUDDING RICE
600ml (1 PINT) MILK
50g (2oz) CASTER SUGAR
ZEST OF ½ LEMON
1 CINNAMON STICK, 1 BAY LEAF AND 1 VANILLA POD, TIED TOGETHER

50g (2oz) SOFT BROWN SUGAR
50g (2 oz) DRIED APRICOTS, SOAKED OVERNIGHT IN 300ml (½ PINT) WATER

Put all the ingredients except the soft brown sugar and the apricots in a pan, bring to the boil, then simmer for about 40 minutes, stirring constantly, until the rice is well cooked and the liquid has thickened. If you haven't got a vanilla pod, never mind. Use a vanilla stick or a little sachet of vanilla powder or a couple of drops of vanilla essence.

Put the apricots in a small dish in a medium oven until the water has virtually disappeared and become a very thick syrup. Chop them. Remove the bundle of herbs and spices from the rice, stir in the apricots and allow to cool, stirring occasionally. Put in a serving bowl or separate ramekin dishes, and refrigerate for a couple of hours.

Finally, sprinkle with the soft brown sugar and glaze under a very, very hot grill.

Alternatively, for fun and games, spread the rice pudding on a plate, sprinkle with the soft brown sugar, and caramelise with a blow-torch. It's best to do this out of sight. People can get a bit peculiar.

PAUL HODGSON
WALTONS

Waltons is tucked away in that posh neck of the woods behind Beauchamp Place. On Walton Street, curiously enough. It was an ordinary enough afternoon when I bicycled over there. Nothing very much happened on the way. Nobody tried to run me over. No thunderstorms soaked me to the skin. I stopped at a tobacconist on the way home and ate a Snickers bar. That was about it, really.

Waltons itself belongs to the yellow swags-and-swathes-and-flounced-curtains school of décor with little lamps on every table – comfy and peaceful in a Knightsbridge bordello sort of way. And Paul Hodgson is a pleasant young Yorkshireman cast in the Strong and Silent mould who worked his way up through Robert Carrier's restaurant in Islington when Gunther Schlender was the head chef. The cooking world is like the Chancery Bar – everybody seems to know everybody else.

If Paul Hodgson is a superlative chef, his spelling is even more spectacular. And I thought *my* spelling was bad. He tells you to 'swet' the onions with a pinch of 'safron'. You use 'spinich' which you drain through a large 'culinder'. You 'serv' them. You add chopped 'vegatables' with a pinch of 'tyme' and you soak 'flagotle' beans. The other day my three-year-old daughter finally learnt to say 'finished' instead of 'fishioned', and I felt a distinct loss. So thank God for his spelling: it servs as an exampel to us all.

And then there's his seafood sausage. Like the prune and armagnac mousse elsewhere, of course it has no place in this book – not even with the best will in the world could it honestly be described as cheap. Unless perhaps you served it as a main course, and this is a cheap version of it made with salmon and mussels rather than scallops and lobster. But it's something so wonderful that it's here in the true spirit of what-the-hell.

RAGOUT OF MUSSELS AND SPINACH

1 ONION, FINELY CHOPPED	2kg (4½lb) MUSSELS, WASHED – THROW
25g (1oz) BUTTER	AWAY ANY WITH
120ml (4fl oz) DRY WHITE WINE	BROKEN SHELLS
PINCH OF SAFFRON	600ml (1 PINT) DOUBLE CREAM
1 BAY LEAF	450g (1lb) SPINACH, WASHED, WITH STALKS REMOVED

Sweat the onion gently in the butter without colouring for 5 minutes. Add the white wine, saffron and bay leaf. Turn up the heat, add the mussels, stir, put a lid on and keep cooking until all the shells have opened.

Drain the mussels into a colander, retaining the liquor for the sauce. Shell the mussels, except for a few which you keep for decoration.

To make the sauce, reduce the liquor down by two-thirds, add the cream and bring to the boil.

Place the washed spinach in a large pan and cook until soft. Add the mussels and stir. Then add the sauce, bring to the boil and serve, with a few mussels in their shells to garnish.

PAN-FRIED NUGGETS OF LAMB WITH THOSE FLAGOTTLE BEANS

2.2 kg (5lb) MIDDLE NECK OF LAMB
3 TABLESPOONS OLIVE OIL
2 CARROTS
2 ONIONS
2 CELERY STALKS
2 GARLIC CLOVES
1 SPRIG EACH OF FRESH THYME AND ROSEMARY
1 TABLESPOON TOMATO PURÉE
½ BOTTLE RED WINE
450g (1lb) DRIED FLAGEOLET BEANS, SOAKED OVERNIGHT

Remove the lamb from the bone. Trim and cut into nuggets.

Brown the bones with 2 tablespoons of olive oil in a hot oven, 220°C/425°F/gas 8, for 20 minutes. Then place them in a pot with 1.2 litres (2 pints) of water, the chopped vegetables and herbs, the tomato purée and the red wine. Bring to the boil and simmer gently for 3 hours, reducing gradually until what you have left is a pint of sauce in the form of a reduced stock. Leave to cool, refrigerate overnight and remove any fat that congeals and hardens on the surface.

The following day, cook the soaked beans in water until they're tender and drain. Meanwhile, sauté the lamb nuggets in the rest of the olive oil, making sure they're still pink inside, add the sauce and serve with the beans.

SEAFOOD SAUSAGES WITH A CREAM AND WHITE WINE SAUCE

450g (1lb) FILLET OF
SALMON
4 EGG WHITES
SALT
PINCH OF CAYENNE
PEPPER
FRESH PARSLEY AND
CHIVES, TARRAGON,
OR DILL TO TASTE
600ml (1 PINT)
DOUBLE CREAM
2 SMALL CHOPPED
SHALLOTS
25g (1oz) BUTTER
1 SMALL BAG
OF MUSSELS IN
THEIR SHELLS
½ BOTTLE
WHITE WINE
175g (6oz) SMOKED
HADDOCK
175g (6oz) WHITE
FISH
SAUSAGE
SKINS
125g (4oz)
BREADCRUMBS

Skin and fillet the salmon, and put it through a blender with the egg whites. Add salt, cayenne pepper, the chopped herbs, and half the cream.

Meanwhile, sweat the shallots in the butter until transparent. Add the mussels which you've scrubbed clean, removing any little hairy beards and jettisoning any mussels with broken shells. Add the white wine, turn up the heat, stir and cover. Cook until all the mussels have opened – being careful not to cook longer than is strictly necessary. Remove the mussels from the shells, retaining the liquor. Chop the mussels roughly, add the roughly chopped smoked haddock and the white fish and mix them all up with the salmon mousse mixture.

Soak a length of sausage skin – say, 1 metre (3ft) – then slip it over a tap and run water through to straighten the skin out and get rid of any excess salt. (Sausage skins are preserved in salt.) Tie one end of the skin and pipe in the mixture. Then tie up the other end and, using a few bits of string, divide the sausages into the individual lengths you fancy. Poach the sausage, bent round and round, in simmering water for 5 minutes, then plunge it into cold water. Remove the sausage skin and roll each sausage in breadcrumbs.

Meanwhile, add the cream to the mussel liquor with whatever herbs take your fancy – again, fresh parsley and chives, or tarragon, or dill – and adjust the seasoning. Keep warm.

Place the sausages under the grill until golden brown, and serve on a bed of diced leeks and carrots surrounded by the sauce.

Hey ho.

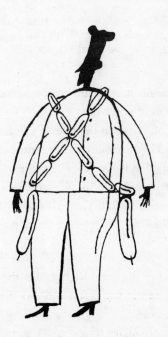

BAKED APPLE AND FRANZIPAN TART

6 EATING APPLES, PEELED, CORED AND FINELY SLICED	JUICE OF 1 LEMON
450g (1lb) PUFF PASTRY, CUT INTO 6 × 10cm (4in) ROUNDS	ICING SUGAR, FOR DUSTING

FOR THE FRANZIPAN

175g (6oz) GROUND ALMONDS
50g (2oz) BUTTER
75g (3oz) SUGAR
2 EGG YOLKS

To make the franzipan, whiz the almonds, butter, sugar and egg yolks in a blender until you have a paste.

Place a blob of franzipan the size of a walnut in the centre of each pastry round. Then arrange two concentric circles of apple slices (which you've dipped in lemon juice to prevent them colouring) on top of the pastry and over, repeat over, the franzipan.

Preheat the oven to 220°C/425°F/gas 7. Dust the tart with icing sugar and bake for 20 minutes until golden brown. Serve with cream.

PHILIP HOWARD
THE SQUARE

I went to see Philip Howard at the Square, opposite Christies, at five
o'clock in the afternoon. The place had that wonderful atmosphere
of people relaxing. Nobody asked in accusing tones if they could
help me – it was as if everybody had been lying in the hot sun all
afternoon. Dazed and benign and soporific. One waiter was on the
floor fiddling with a screwdriver and a light. 'The kitchen? Down
the stairs, door on the right.' I walked past the cash till, where a
girl was eating an early supper, reading a magazine and answering
the telephone. 'You want Philip? I'm not sure he's in. Try anyway
– down the stairs.' Down the stairs beside the kitchen was a small,
ugly room with carved stucco flowers on the walls. A waiter and a
waitress were sitting at a table discussing GCSEs. Someone else sat
in the corner eating supper. 'Philip went to the bank,' said one of
them. 'He should be back soon,' said another. A sous chef appeared
from the kitchen. 'Philip? He went out,' he said. 'Have a seat,' said
someone else. 'Have some coffee.'

In the event, I wandered out to buy a copy of Claudia Roden's
Middle Eastern Cookery. Past Christies, past dealers selling old masters,
past one shop selling cigars and another selling those hats that people
only ever wear at race-courses. Past Fortnums. Up three flights of
stairs in Hatchards, down the stairs again and back to the Square.

'Philip rang, he's on his way,' said the girl at the cash register.
I wandered downstairs. 'He'll be here soon,' said the waitress who'd
been discussing GCSEs. Two minutes later, he came bounding
down the stairs two at a time in a white sweater, out of breath,
arms outstretched in greeting. Not many chefs look like chefs, but
Philip Howard doesn't even begin to look like a chef – he looks

like a tennis player, the one the mothers swoon over and dote on at Wimbledon.

But there's no question, he definitely is a chef. In fact, he couldn't be more of a chef if he tried. He's worked with the Roux brothers and he's worked with Marco Pierre White and he's worked at Bibendum – in terms of culinary pedigree, you can't get much more thoroughbred than that.

'Have you always cooked?'

'No. Only when I left university.'

'Oh? What did you study?'

'Microbiology.'

PISSALADIÈRE (INDIVIDUAL PIZZAS WITH ONION, OLIVE AND ANCHOVY)

FOR THE DOUGH

15g (½oz) FRESH YEAST	1 EGG
75ml (2½fl oz) WARM WATER	250g (9oz) FLOUR
½ TEASPOON SUGAR	¾ TEASPOON SALT
	1 TABLESPOON OLIVE OIL

FOR THE TOPPING

6 SPANISH ONIONS	1 GARLIC CLOVE
1 TABLESPOON OLIVE OIL	1 TIN ANCHOVY FILLETS
50g (2oz) BUTTER	30 BLACK OLIVES, STONED
SALT AND PEPPER	

Combine the yeast and water by rubbing between your fingers. Add the sugar and gently whisk in the egg. Make a well in the flour, add the salt, the yeast-and-water mixture, and the oil. Knead for a few minutes until you have a smooth, elastic dough. Let it sit in a warm place for an hour.

Meanwhile, peel and slice the onions and sweat them slowly for half an hour over a low heat in a mixture of oil and butter. Add salt and pepper to taste, and sweat for another half an hour until the onions are soft and golden. At the last moment, crush a clove of garlic beneath the blade of a heavy knife and stir into the onions. Drain in a colander to remove any excess oil.

Preheat the oven to 230°C/450°F/gas 8. Divide the dough into balls and roll out into separate pizza bases. Spread a thin layer of onion over each base, then arrange the anchovies and the olives in a lattice on top, and bake in the preheated oven for 15 minutes.

FRESH PASTA WITH RABBIT AND MUSTARD

1 RABBIT	900ml (1½ pints)
1 TABLESPOON OIL	CHICKEN STOCK (SEE
1 CELERY STALK	BELOW)
1 SMALL LEEK	A BOUQUET
5 LARGE ONIONS	GARNI
1 CARROT	2 TABLESPOONS
75g (3oz) BUTTER	GRAIN MUSTARD
SALT AND	300ml (½ PINT)
FRESHLY GROUND	DOUBLE CREAM
BLACK PEPPER	6 PORTIONS OF
	FRESH PASTA

Cut the rabbit in 4, then fry in oil until golden.

In another pan, sweat the chopped celery, the leek, 1 onion and the carrot in half the butter. Season with salt and pepper. Add the rabbit, cover with the chicken stock, throw in the bouquet garni, bring the whole lot to the boil, and simmer gently for 1½ hours, until the meat is falling off the bone.

129

Leave to cool, then remove the meat from the bone. Pass the liquid through a sieve and reduce to approximately 300ml (½ pint).

Meanwhile, thinly slice and sweat the other 4 onions in the rest of the butter until golden. Season to taste with salt and pepper. Add the rabbit meat, the reduced stock, the mustard and the cream, bring to the boil and pour over the fresh pasta, which you've been cunningly cooking in the meantime.

Note: The chicken stock can be made from a stock cube or bought at a supermarket. Because the mustard has such a strong flavour, it doesn't really need to be fresh. On the other hand, fresh stock is always preferable. So if you've got the time and the energy, take a few chicken wings or a couple of carcasses. Add a carrot, a stalk of celery, a medium-sized onion, a small leek – all roughly chopped – to 1.2 litres (a couple of pints) of water. Throw in a bouquet garni and simmer away for a couple of hours.

TARTE FINE DES BANANES

225g (8oz) PUFF   6 RIPE BANANAS
PASTRY   ICING SUGAR

Preheat the oven to 180°C/350°F/gas 4.

Roll out the puff pastry into six 15cm (6in) discs, about 2mm (¹⁄₁₆in) thick. With a fork, prick all over, except around the edge. Slice the bananas on the diagonal, about 0.5cm (¼in) thick. Arrange, overlapping, in concentric circles until the disc is covered. Dust with icing sugar and bake for 20 minutes, until golden. Serve with cream. (And if you just happen to have a slurp of rum in the cream, so much the better. But utterly unnecessary.)

PETER KROMBERG
LE SOUFFLÉ

Another kindly German. Instead of just saying he was far too busy to see me, he arranged a time two months further on, immediately after Christmas. 'I'm sorry,' he said 'but it's the first free moment I've got.'

Peter Kromberg is the chef at Le Soufflé in the Inter Continental Hotel at Hyde Park Corner, which recently won the Egon Ronay Restaurant of the Year award. Like Gunther Schlender, I can easily imagine him peering into your mouth with a drill in his hand and saying, 'Just raise your hand when you want me to stop.' But take any middle-aged man with a certain *gravitas* immaculately dressed in starched whites and your thoughts are bound to turn to dentistry.

Mr Kromberg is clearly much liked. During the brief period I was sitting in his office, there were many interruptions. A celebrated chef from Strasbourg dropped in to see him. Someone else gave him a late Christmas present. Good wishes came buzzing thick and fast down the telephone. The air was foggy with kindness.

He explained how you go about winning the Restaurant of the Year award. I hadn't realised it was so easy. You obviously have to be highly organised, but then thousands of people are highly organised. Then you have to have the perfect set-up: different kitchens for different purposes, rather than one central monolith which deals with everything from room service to banquets. So – a few functional kitchens. No problem. This is where it starts to get a little more tricky. You have to serve consistently creative, innovative food using nothing but the very best ingredients served in the right quantity at a reasonable price. Part and parcel of the same thing, you need to have a lifetime's knowledge of choosing and cooking

131

ingredients appropriate to the season. This tends to involve years of learning from other people and gradually branching off to develop your own style.

Next, you have to have a smoothly functioning team behind you: not only in the kitchen, but between the chefs and the waiters. No wars. No internecine conflicts. Waiters and chefs have to help each other out when everything starts hitting the fan. And finally, you need to know how to deal with people, often under considerable stress.

He learnt how to treat people when in his early twenties, working with a highly volatile staff in Asia. There, one word out of place, even a simple misunderstanding, and a chef is quite likely to respond by tearing off his jacket, hurling it on to the charcoal grill and storming out, throwing away years of experience to become a taxi driver in Bangkok. This actually happened, and he's been kind to people ever since. You never, ever – for example – reprimand anybody in front of somebody else.

Do all this, day in, day out, and you might stand a fair chance of being considered for Egon Ronay's award. Like I said, a doddle.

And the funny thing is, Peter Kromberg never wanted to be a chef in the first place. His father died when he was ten weeks old and his mother didn't have enough money to pay for college fees. He wanted to be a forester.

BROCCOLI SOUFFLÉ WITH ALMONDS AND TAPENADE

SALT, FRESHLY
GROUND BLACK
PEPPER AND
NUTMEG
600ml (1 PINT) MILK
2½oz (60g) BUTTER
3 EGG YOLKS (KEEP
THE WHITES) AND 2
WHOLE EGGS
3oz (75g) FLOUR

3oz (75g) CHEESE
2oz (50g) FLAKED
ROASTED ALMONDS
450g (1lb) BROCCOLI
(HEADS ONLY),
BOILED AND PURÉED
6 EGG WHITES
1oz (25g) FLAKED
PLAIN ALMONDS

Preheat the oven to 160°C/325°F/gas 3.

To make the basic soufflé mixture, add seasoning to the milk and bring three-quarters of the milk and the butter to the boil.

Mix the whole eggs, yolks and flour with the remaining cold milk and add slowly to the boiling milk.

Turn the heat down very low. When the mixture thickens, remove from the heat and add the cheese.

Mix the roasted almonds into this mixture and add the puréed broccoli.

Whip the egg whites until stiff and fold gently into the mixture.

Pour into buttered dishes sprinkled well with flour or grated cheese.

Sprinkle flaked almonds on top.

Cook in the preheated oven for 30–45 minutes.

THE TAPENADE

2½oz (60g) STONED BLACK OLIVES
1 TEASPOON WASHED CAPERS
1oz (25g) ANCHOVIES
1 TEASPOON STRONG MUSTARD
1 DESSERTSPOON OLIVE OIL
SALT AND FRESHLY GROUND BLACK PEPPER
JUICE OF ½ LEMON

Mix the olives, capers and anchovies together with a pestle and mortar until you have a paste. Add the mustard and gradually add the olive oil, until you get a sauce-like texture. Season with salt, pepper and lemon juice.

VEGETABLE STRUDEL WITH WATERCRESS AND RED CAPSICUM SAUCE

1 MEDIUM SAVOY CABBAGE
150g (5oz) BUTTER
4 COOKED CARROTS
½ CELERIAC, COOKED AND CUT INTO THICK BATONS
125g (4oz) COOKED BUTTON MUSHROOMS
125g (4oz) COOKED BROCCOLI FLOWERETS
1 TOMATO, PEELED, DE-SEEDED AND CUT INTO WEDGES
125g (4oz) COOKED AND SEASONED SPINACH
SEA SALT AND FRESHLY GROUND BLACK PEPPER
CARAWAY SEEDS

Blanch the outer leaves of the cabbage and cool.

Cut the inside into chunks, put in a pot with half the butter and 150ml (5fl oz) of water. Cook until tender and all the liquid has gone.

Lay the large cabbage leaves on a cheesecloth and fill as you wish with all the vegetables in layers.

Sprinkle with salt, pepper and caraway seeds, wrap the leaves around and roll up in the muslin.

Tie each end with string, with an extra piece of string tied round the middle. Lay the strudel on a rack in a roasting tin half-filled with water, cover with foil, and steam over a medium heat for about 45 minutes.

To serve, remove the strudel from the steamer and unwrap the cheesecloth. Cut the strudel into thick slices, and serve on a large, hot dish with the sauces on each side.

WATERCRESS SAUCE

2 BUNCHES WATERCRESS, STALKS REMOVED	50g (2oz) BUTTER SALT AND FRESHLY GROUND
200ml (7fl oz) WATER	BLACK PEPPER
2 TABLESPOONS DOUBLE CREAM	

Place the washed cress in a saucepan. Add the water and cream and cook for 12 minutes, covered. Put in a liquidiser with the butter. Blend until smooth. Season and keep warm.

RED CAPSICUM SAUCE

50g (2oz) BUTTER	200ml (7fl oz)
1/4 ONION, CHOPPED	DOUBLE CREAM
2 RED PEPPERS, WASHED, PIPPED AND QUARTERED	SALT AND FRESHLY GROUND BLACK PEPPER
300ml (10fl oz) WATER	

Heat half the butter in a saucepan. Add the onion and peppers and sweat for a few minutes. Add the water and cook slowly for 10 minutes. Add the cream and cook for another 15 minutes. Pour into a liquidiser. Add the remaining butter. Season and keep warm.

A MOUSSE OF CURD CHEESE

225g (8oz) SUGAR	600ml (1 PINT)
1 TABLESPOON	WHIPPING CREAM
VANILLA SUGAR	10 EGG WHITES
450g (1lb) CURD	ZEST OF 1 LEMON
CHEESE, QUARK	
OR PHILADELPHIA	
CREAM CHEESE	

Mix half the sugar with the vanilla sugar, cheese and lemon zest. Fold in the whipped cream. Whip the egg whites with the rest of the sugar and fold into the mixture. Pour the mixture into muslin and hang up to drain for 4 hours.

Garnish with redcurrants at the side.

Rowley Leigh
Kensington Place

Rowley Leigh is one of those people that the headmaster at school wouldn't have been quite sure how to deal with. The choice would be expelling him for the usual things (drinking, smoking, betting and having a go at the matron's daughter, all during the run-up to exams), or else making him head boy and hoping the school stayed out of the pages of the *News of the World*.

What happened – in this wholly imaginary scenario – was that Rowley Leigh was in fact made head boy and proved a popular choice. The Fourth Form admired him because it was all a bit like Jimi Hendrix becoming Home Secretary, and the headmaster was praised for his insight and eventually short-listed for the headmastership of Eton.

When Leigh left school, people lost track of him. Someone said he was in Marseilles. Someone else met someone who'd got a postcard from him in Guadalajara. There were rumours about a misunderstanding over a credit card in Geneva. A second cousin said they'd heard he was working in a kitchen.

Then – and this is the only true part of the story – Kensington Place opened in 1987 with Rowley Leigh as the chef. It was towards the end of that awful period when Mrs Thatcher wanted us all to become Japanese and people were still suffering the after-effects of cuisine minceur. Along comes Leigh and says, 'Sod this for a lark,' or words to the effect, and dishes up food that can be eaten as well as photographed. Kensington Place has been packed ever since.

When I met him, Rowley Leigh was in particularly good form. He'd just had a successful evening playing poker with Charles Fontaine from the Quality Chop House the night before, and was lasciviously anticipating an interview with *Vogue* later that afternoon.

AUBERGINE CAVIAR

6 AUBERGINES
4 TABLESPOONS
OLIVE OIL PLUS
EXTRA TO BRUSH
AUBERGINES
FRESHLY GROUND
BLACK PEPPER
12 BLACK OLIVES,
FINELY CHOPPED

3 GARLIC CLOVES,
FINELY CHOPPED
8 ANCHOVY FILLETS,
FINELY CHOPPED
2 TABLESPOONS
CHIVES, FINELY
CHOPPED

Halve the aubergines, sprinkle them with salt, and leave them in a colander to drain for an hour.

Preheat the oven to 220°C/425°F/gas 7. Brush the aubergines with olive oil, season with freshly ground black pepper, and bake in the oven for 40 minutes or until they're completely tender.

Scrape the flesh into a colander and press well to extract any liquid. Coarsely chop the pulp, then mix in the olives, garlic, anchovy fillets, chives and 4 tablespoons olive oil.

Cover and refrigerate. Serve with toast, pitta bread or blinis.

ROAST COD WITH MUSTARD GRAVY

FOR THE GRAVY

1 LARGE ONION, FINELY CHOPPED
2 CARROTS, FINELY CHOPPED
2 CELERY STALKS, FINELY CHOPPED
FISH HEAD (OR HEADS)
1 GARLIC CLOVE, FINELY CHOPPED
1 SPRING OF THYME
1 BAY LEAF
6 PEPPERCORNS
1 DESSERTSPOON FLOUR

1 TEASPOON TOMATO PURÉE
600ml (1 PINT) WATER (OR WHITE WINE, OR HALF WATER/HALF WINE)
BUTTER FOR FRYING, AND 50g (2oz) BUTTER FOR STIRRING INTO THE SAUCE
2 TEASPOONS STRONG ENGLISH MUSTARD
SALT

FOR THE ROAST COD

6 THICK COD FILLETS
50g (2oz) FLOUR, WELL SEASONED

OIL AND BUTTER FOR FRYING

Fry the onion, carrot and celery with the fish head in a little butter until well coloured. Add the garlic, thyme, bayleaf and peppercorns. Sprinkle with ½ a dessertspoon of flour and cook until it, too, is well coloured. Then add the tomato purée and the wine and/or water. Bring to the boil and simmer, uncovered, for half an hour, skimming well, allowing it to reduce. Then drain through a sieve and whisk in the butter and mustard. Season with salt and a squeeze of lemon juice.

Preheat the oven to 230°C/450°F/gas 8.

Dredge the cod fillets through the flour. Heat the oil and butter until very hot in a frying pan, then quickly brown the cod fillets on both sides. Transfer to the preheated oven for 3 or 4 minutes, until the cod is just cooked.

Serve immediately with mashed potatoes and plenty of gravy.

FLOATING ISLANDS WITH CUSTARD

8 VERY FRESH EGGS 1 VANILLA POD (OR
225g (8oz) SUGAR   A FEW DROPS OF
600ml (1 PINT) MILK   VANILLA ESSENCE)
                                A SQUEEZE OF
                                LEMON JUICE

Separate the eggs. Whisk the yolks with half the sugar. Heat the milk to boiling point with the vanilla pod or the essence, then pour it over the beaten egg yolks, whisking all the while. Return the mixture to the saucepan and cook very gently on the stove, stirring constantly, until the custard thickens sufficiently to coat the back of a spoon. Remove immediately and allow to cool.

Whisk the whites, preferably with an electric whisk, slowly adding the remaining sugar and a little lemon juice until the whites become a stiff and glossy meringue.

With a pair of serving spoons, form the meringue into large egg shapes and then poach in simmering water for between 2 and 3 minutes on each side. Drain on a cloth.

Make a caramel by browning some sugar in a pan and diluting it with a few drops of water. Drizzle this over the floating islands, which you serve on a sea of custard.

DES MCDONALD
THE IVY

The Ivy – more or less slap bang in the epicentre of the West End – has been around since 1911, although its present reincarnation is considerably more recent. It is currently basking in giddy fame and popularity. Terence Conran once described it as his favourite London restaurant, and so far as I know he isn't even a shareholder.

I got off my bike and wandered around outside in the dark in the pouring rain, feeling like a tramp as I peered through the windows at the warm glow inside, all silver and soft lights. By definition, that's what luxury restaurants are for – a temporary refuge from all the pushing and the shoving, the grime, the wet and the hard chairs. And here's a luxury restaurant – almost the quintessence of luxury restaurants – bursting at the seams just before Christmas, with an army of chefs and waiters working flat out, that is prepared to let in a bedraggled wreck with a soggy notebook and talk about cheap food. How, I wonder, did the Iron Curtain last as long as it did?

ROASTED AUBERGINE SOUP WITH PIQUILLO RELISH

1.4kg (3lb) AUBERGINES
1 GARLIC CLOVE
FRESH OR DRIED THYME
1–2 LEEKS
BUTTER
50g (2oz) FLOUR
25g (1oz) ROASTED CUMIN SEEDS
1 RED CHILLI, FINELY CHOPPED
1 BAY LEAF
1.7 litres (3 PINTS) VEGETABLE OR MILD CHICKEN STOCK

Preheat the oven to 200°C/400°F/gas 6.

Cut the aubergines in half and score the flesh. Rub with the chopped garlic, scatter with thyme and bake in the preheated oven for half an hour.

Sweat the leeks slowly in the butter in a saucepan, without colouring, and dust with flour. The flour is to act as a binding agent rather than a thickening one. Add the cumin seeds, chilli, bay leaf and stock, bring to the boil and simmer for 20 minutes.

Add the cooked aubergine, blend and correct the seasoning. Garnish with a spoonful of piquillo relish.

THE PIQUILLO RELISH

2 RED PEPPERS
1 SHALLOT, FINELY
CHOPPED
1 TABLESPOON
CHOPPED BASIL
1 TABLESPOON
CHOPPED
CORIANDER

2 TABLESPOONS
OLIVE OIL
1 TEASPOON
CHILLI SAUCE
SALT

Cut the peppers in half and grill them until the skin darkens. Pop them in a bag until cool, then peel and chop them finely. (Putting them in a bag makes them easier to peel.) Add the other ingredients and mix together.

POT ROAST OF PORK BELLY WITH CIDER, LENTILS AND SAUTÉD APPLES

1.4kg (3lb)
PORK BELLY
2 GARLIC CLOVES
FRESH OR DRIED
THYME
1 BAY LEAF
1 TABLESPOON
ALLSPICE
4 CLOVES
1 BOTTLE SWEET
CIDER
1 VEGETABLE
STOCK CUBE
A CHICKEN CARCASS,
OR A HANDFUL OF
CHICKEN WINGS

1.4kg (3 lb) OF ANY
ROOT VEGETABLES
TO HAND (LEEKS,
TURNIPS, PARSNIPS,
CARROTS, CELERY)
1 TEASPOON OF
TOMATO PURÉE
350g (12oz) LENTILS,
SOAKED OVERNIGHT
1.4kg (3lb) COOKING
APPLES
125g (4oz) SUGAR
125g (4oz) BUTTER

Boil the belly of pork for 1 hour in water to cover, with the garlic, thyme, bay leaf, allspice, cloves, cider and vegetable stock cube. It produces a marvellous, heady brew. Remove the pork and reduce the liquor to a pint.

Meanwhile, make a brown chicken stock. Brown the chicken bones and/or the wings and the root vegetables in a high oven for 20 minutes or so, then simmer them in 1.2 litres (2 pints) of water with the tomato purée for a couple of hours. Strain and reduce to 600ml (1 pint) of stock. Preheat the oven to 200°C/400°F/gas 6.

Slash the skin of the pork belly crossways with a very sharp knife into a latticework of diamonds. Combine the two reduced stocks. Lay the pork on a bed of lentils in a casserole dish and pour over the stock. The skin of the pork should remain above the stock and crispen, whereas the meat actually poaches in the stock. Cook in the

143

preheated oven for an hour or so, basting from time to time, until the skin is golden brown and crispy and the lentils are cooked.

Peel, core and slice the apples. Caramelise the sugar and the butter, then fry the apples in it until they're soft and have taken on colour. Serve with the pork.

ORANGE AND SAFFRON RISOTTO

300ml (½ PINT) STOCK SYRUP (MADE WITH SUGAR, WATER, JUICE OF A LEMON, A CLOVE AND A CINNAMON STICK) 175g (6oz) ARBORIO OR CARNAROLLI RICE	50g (2oz) BUTTER 300ml (½ PINT) ORANGE JUICE 1 LITTLE SACHET SAFFRON 1 SMALL CARTON DOUBLE CREAM A HANDFUL OF SULTANAS ZEST OF 1 ORANGE

To make the stock syrup, bring to the boil equal parts of water and sugar with the lemon juice, clove and cinnamon and simmer for half an hour. Strain.

Stir the rice in the butter in a frying pan on a very low heat until transparent. Then add, little by little, the heated stock syrup and orange juice, along with the saffron, stirring all the while. The rice should never swim in the liquid – always add a little at a time.

When the risotto is ready, stir in the double cream and a handful of sultanas, and garnish with strips of orange zest that have been blanched in boiling water.

If you're serving it cold, sprinkle it with brown sugar and bang it under a very, very hot grill.

RICHARD WALTON
CHEZ MOI

Richard Walton is a patriarch among chefs. He predates Mrs Thatcher. He originally came to England from Rhodesia, before it became Zimbabwe, even before Ian Smith and his Declaration of Independence. (This was at the time of a man called Harold Wilson, a bloke with a pipe and a dodgy grasp of economics.) He was a management trainee at the Savoy for seven years, until they sent him to Lausanne, where he suddenly realised he preferred cooking to anything in the hotel business.

He's cooked at Chez Moi for almost thirty years and looks back nostalgically to the days when the food was brought to your table on a trolley. 'The trolley went up and down the restaurant. The customers started with an empty plate and chose exactly what they wanted. The waiters would carve the meat expertly in front of them. There was hustle and bustle and activity. For middle-aged couples bored with each other's company, it was theatre and entertainment.'

Chez Moi is in deepest, richest Holland Park. The warm fug of money hits you the moment you walk through the door. People still go there wearing furs. The waiters are patrician. None of the staff smell – there's a notice in the kitchen which says: 'Body odours are a sign of a lack of hygiene and are offensive to others. Anyone noticed to be lax in the field will be notified as politely as possible and expected to rectify the situation.' Richard Walton's partners, he told me, were worried that cooking on the cheap was not the kind of image the restaurant should be promoting.

The trouble is, he's another of these naturally kind people. He clearly can't help it, so the warnings of his partners went unheeded. He was tired the afternoon we met – Fay Maschler had been in the previous evening and Michael Winner had just finished a three-course lunch followed by coffee inside an hour. But within minutes he was showing me salmon in the various stages of curing; fresh turmeric ('It's much better than the ground stuff. I'll wrap some up for you. Make sure you don't get it on your fingers because it's hell to get off'); plunging his hand into the garbage to show me the residue of spices that went into the Thai chicken ('You have to get rid of all this stuff. You can't put it in a liquidiser – it's too tough to tenderise'); handing me packets of satay spice ('Go on, take it. It might take you a couple of days to get hold of some').

And he gave me some of the Thai chicken to taste, so delicious that it almost punches you, and well worth the effort of finding a Thai shop that will sell you the curry paste, the fresh turmeric and the Kaffir lime leaves. 'A lot of research, a lot of testing went into developing it,' he says.

GRAVALAD LAX

900g (2lb) FILLETED TAIL OF SALMON	8 BAY LEAVES
2 TABLESPOONS BROWN SUGAR	1 BUNCH OF CHOPPED DILL
2 TEASPOONS SALT	1 TABLESPOON SOY SAUCE
2 TEASPOONS CRUSHED BLACK PEPPERCORNS	1 TABLESPOON BRANDY (VERY OPTIONAL)

Stretch out a sheet of clingfilm on the table. Scatter half the ingredients on to the clingfilm (except for the soy sauce and brandy) and lay the salmon on top, with its skin side down.

Repeat the process, scattering the other half of the ingredients on top of the salmon. Pour over the soy sauce, and the brandy if you happen to have some knocking around the house. Cover with the clingfilm round it, then put it on a tray or a dish under a piece of wood weighed down with a couple of bricks for 4 days at the bottom of the fridge. You can take it out and throw away the juices.

Carve like smoked salmon and serve with thin brown bread and butter. (Some people insist on mustard and dill sauce with it, which is gilding the lily.)

THAI CHICKEN

1 CHICKEN	1 TEASPOON GREEN
1 ONION	OR RED THAI
125g (4oz) GINGER	CURRY PASTE
4 GARLIC CLOVES	1 TABLESPOON
1 RED CHILLI	PEANUT BUTTER
2 PIECES OF FRESH	1 TABLESPOON
TURMERIC (EACH	HONEY
5cm/2in LONG) OR	1 TIN COCONUT
A PINCH OF GROUND	MILK
TURMERIC)	150ml (5fl oz)
ZEST OF ½ LIME	WHIPPING CREAM
50g (2oz) DRY	1 SMALL TUB OF
SATAY SPICE MIX	THICK GREEK
(OPTIONAL)	YOGHURT
4 SPRIGS OF	FRESH CORIANDER
LEMON GRASS	TO GARNISH
6 KAFFIR LIME	
LEAVES	

Skin and bone the chicken and cut into cubes.

Peel and chop what needs to be peeled or chopped, then put all the ingredients except for the chicken and coriander into a saucepan, bring gently to the boil and simmer for half an hour.

Add the cubes of chicken and cook gently for another 20 minutes. Let it cool, then remove the chicken pieces and put the sauce through a mouli or a sieve to remove the hard spices. And in a perfect world, let the whole thing sit overnight for the flavours to develop fully.

Reheat, garnish with fresh coriander and serve with plain boiled rice.

PINEAPPLE SATURN

1 TABLESPOON HONEY	6 SCOOPS VANILLA ICE CREAM
50g (2oz) SUGAR	1 TEASPOON
JUICE OF 4 ORANGES	POWDERED
6 SLICES OF FRESH	CINNAMON
PINEAPPLE, PEELED	
AND CORED	

Make a syrup with the honey, sugar and orange juice.

Warm the pineapple in the syrup, and then, when you turn over the pineapple, dust with the cinnamon.

Place a slice of the warm pineapple on each plate with a scoop of vanilla ice cream in the centre and surround with the hot syrup.

BRYAN WEBB

HILAIRE

I met Bryan Webb at Hilaire in the Old Brompton Road at 3.30 in the afternoon, having spent a very curious morning in the City.

I was writing an article for the *Investors Chronicle* on how to become a stockbroker, which involved interviewing the head of the equity sales desk at Société Générale Strauss Turnbull (SGST) in one of those breathtakingly high-tech buildings just behind Liverpool Street. In order not to be late for the interview I'd arrived far too early, so for almost an hour I did what one always does whenever one arrives too early for something. I wandered around gawping at the buildings, watched people hurrying about their business, got colder and colder and generally felt foolish.

The chap I was interviewing at SGST turned out to be frighteningly intelligent, articulate and pleasant – a lethal combination at that time in the morning. And while I was there, the retail trade figures were announced and all hell broke loose – an entire floor of stockbrokers started babbling into telephones in a state of barely controlled hysteria. It was all very exciting. I sat in the Bishopsgate library afterwards, transcribing the taped interview using an earplug. But by the time I'd finished, around lunchtime, I'd suddenly run out of energy. I felt like a deflated balloon, and I wasn't due to meet Bryan Webb for over two hours . . .

So I pedalled down from the City to South Kensington to visit My Friend the Travel Writer, the one who never leaves the house. I arrived in SW10 – Lawrence of Arabia having crossed the desert – with just enough energy left to lean on the bell.

And he wasn't there. I couldn't believe it. I rang the bell over and over again in appalled disbelief. For heaven's sake, he was writing a book about canoeing across Canada – how could he possibly not be at home? I slumped back on my bicycle wondering what on earth to do for the next two hours. I conceived a whole new form of begging: ''Scuse me guv, but could you spare us a bit 'o floor to crash on for a couple of hours?' I peered through the window, dreaming of coffee and laughter.

Then I pedalled off down the road to the Brompton library, where a sign said 'Open. 9am-1 pm' and the doors were firmly shut. Back to the Fulham Road, where I bought a flabby, lukewarm steak and kidney pie and ate it on the street. It coated the roof of my mouth with a quarter of an inch of congealed grease. And then I killed time in the Pan Bookstore, which reinforced my theory that there's nothing in life so exhausting and dispiriting as doing nothing.

When I finally walked through the door of Hilaire, a waiter dropped a huge tray of cutlery to devastating effect. I was ushered downstairs and Bryan came out, a very hot Friar Tuck from the Valleys. 'How can I help you?' he asked. Dread words. Then he asked me what I'd got so far, and I couldn't for the life of me remember a single dish.

'Have you got a paté?' he asked.

'Yes, I was given a paté by . . . by . . . the chap who has that restaurant. It's called . . . the one opposite the *Guardian*.'

'The Quality Chop House?'

'That's it! The Quality Chop House!'

After an awful lot of mental heave-ho-ing and a few silences, we settled on a menu. Afterwards he sent me the recipes.

But consider the following. A man works six days a week running a restaurant – often until one o'clock in the morning. Sunday is his only clear day, which he uses to do the books. A complete stranger walks into his restaurant and sits there in front of him with about as much intellectual spark as a piece of burnt toast. Would you sit down and write out recipes for that stranger on your only day off? Would you?

SALAD OF POACHED SKATE, FRENCH BEANS, POTATOES AND SALSA VERDE

12 SMALL NEW POTATOES	1 LARGE SKATE WING
250g (8oz) FRENCH BEANS	

FOR THE SALSA VERDE

1 BUNCH OF FLAT PARSLEY	25g (1oz) GHERKINS
A FEW SPRIGS OF TARRAGON AND BASIL (OPTIONAL, BUT NICE WORK IF YOU CAN GET IT)	25g (1oz) CAPERS
	25g (1oz) ANCHOVY FILLETS
	2 GARLIC CLOVES
	60ml (2fl oz) OLIVE OIL

Boil the potatoes, then peel and slice. Boil the beans until *al dente*, then refresh under cold water, drain and slice lengthways.

Put all the ingredients for the salsa verde – except for the oil – into a blender. Then trickle in the oil slowly.

Poach the skate for 6 minutes, and remove from the bone. Flake the fish with the potatoes and beans, add the salsa to taste and serve warm.

BRAISED PORK WITH GREMOLATA AND SAFFRON RISOTTO

1.4kg (3lb) BONELESS
SHOULDER OF PORK
4 SHALLOTS
1 LARGE CARROT
2 CELERY STALKS
1 LEEK
ARACHIDE OIL FOR
FRYING
SALT AND
FRESHLY GROUND
BLACK PEPPER

4 GARLIC CLOVES,
CHOPPED
1 LARGE WINEGLASS
WHITE WINE
200g (7oz) TIN OF
TOMATOES
1.2 LITRE (2 PINTS)
CHICKEN STOCK
FRESH OR DRIED
THYME, PARSLEY
STALKS AND 2
BAY LEAVES

FOR THE RISOTTO

600ml (1 PINT)
CHICKEN STOCK
WITH A GOOD PINCH
OF SAFFRON
6 SHALLOTS, FINELY
CHOPPED

200g (7oz) RISOTTO
RICE
SALT AND
FRESHLY GROUND
BLACK PEPPER

FOR THE GREMOLATA

4 GARLIC CLOVES
1 LEMON
1 BUNCH OF FLAT PARSLEY

For the pork: Trim and cube the pork and dice the vegetables. Fry the pork in oil to seal it, season with salt and pepper and put in a large saucepan. Sweat the vegetables and garlic in the same frying pan but do not colour. Add the wine and cook until reduced by half.

Transfer the wine and vegetables into the saucepan with the pork, add the tinned tomatoes, the chicken stock and the herbs and top up with sufficient cold water to cover. Bring to the boil, skim and simmer for an hour.

For the risotto: Bring the chicken stock and saffron to the boil and liquidise. Sweat the finely chopped shallots in a saucepan with a little oil but again, don't colour. Add the rice and the stock, little by little, and season with salt and pepper. Cook slowly on top of the cooker for 15 minutes.

For the gremolata: Mix the crushed garlic, the finely grated lemon rind and the finely chopped parsley.

To finish: Remove the pork pieces from the pan and keep warm. Pass the liquid and vegetables through a sieve and reduce the juices until they thicken slightly. Return the pork to the sauce and stir in the gremolata. Serve with the risotto on the side.

ST EMILION AU CHOCOLAT

175g (6oz) CHOCOLATE	8 AMARETTI BISCUITS
20g (¾oz) BUTTER	1 SMALL WINEGLASS
30ml (1fl oz) DOUBLE CREAM	BRANDY
4 EGGS, SEPARATED	60ml (2fl oz) DOUBLE CREAM, LIGHTLY WHIPPED, TO SERVE

Melt the chocolate with the butter and cream and beat in the egg yolks one by one.

Whisk the egg whites and fold into the chocolate mixture. Crush one biscuit into each of 6 ramekins and add a dash of brandy. Pour on the chocolate mixture, leave to set, and then top lightly with whipped cream and the remaining biscuits, crushed.

TOTALLY ECLECTIC

PAUL BLOXHAM

THE FIRE STATION

After the Fire Station stopped being a fire station and before it became a restaurant, it was the largest squat in London. With its shiny brick walls and tiled floor, the place still looks like a municipal lavatory built on epic proportions, and a lot of work goes into maintaining its distressed edges. Old tables collapse and are lovingly replaced by collapsing old tables. It's bustling and young and noisy, and the whole place is a cheerful exercise in controlled anarchy and pandemonium. But by far the most astonishing thing about the Fire Station is Paul Bloxham.

Most chefs are unusual, but Paul Bloxham is well-nigh unbelievable. It's tiring just to think about him. First thing in the morning, while most people are still fumbling for their coffee and vaguely easing their way into the morning, Paul Bloxham is already behaving like a cross between a magnesium flare and a footballer who's just scored the winning goal in the FA cup final. He's nearly thirty and he looks about sixteen. Before we met, he'd been up until two in the morning digging out recipes for me, so by the time I turned up he had them all written down and costed, page after page. While we were talking, an enormous consignment of sea-bass arrived from Lowestoft that the fish suppliers were virtually giving away. ('Yeees! Nice one! *Nice one!*') His enthusiasm is humbling. He was enthusiastic about working with marinades, about braising and slow cooking and all the various ways of gradually adding flavour to cheap cuts of meat. He was enthusiastic about other chefs. He was even enthusiastic about working for a large company – the Fire Station is owned by Regent Inns. 'People say working for a big company takes the edge off. It doesn't. It just makes everything work more efficiently.'

But a person has to relax, and Bloxham's idea of gentle relaxation is taking part in international cooking contests. There's a competition run by the Epicurean World Master Chef Society in Limoges, where teams of ten chefs from various countries compete with each other. They are presented with a box of unknown ingredients at eight in the morning and given ten hours to prepare a seven-course banquet including bread, petits fours, canapés and centrepieces. In the past five years, Paul Bloxham and the British team have won it three times. The lads done good.

GRILLED MACKEREL BRUSCETTA WITH TAPENADE

125g (4oz) PITTED BLACK OLIVES	3 MACKEREL, FILLETED (6 FILLETS)
2 GARLIC CLOVES	6 EGGS, HARD-BOILED
3–4 TABLESPOONS OLIVE OIL	2 TABLESPOONS PARSLEY
1 LOAF DAY-OLD CIABBATA BREAD	1 LEMON

To make the tapenade, put the olives and anchovies and 1 garlic clove into a liquidiser and blend. Then slowly drip in 2 tablespoons of olive oil until you get a creamy paste.

Cut the bread at an angle to get 6 longer pieces. Rub the bread with the second clove of garlic, brush with olive oil and then toast.

Brush the mackerel with oil, then grill for about 2 minutes on each side, starting with the skin side down.

Spread the tapenade on the bread, lay the mackerel on top, scatter first with the chopped egg, then the parsley, and finally trickle a little extra olive oil on top. Serve with a wedge of lemon at the side.

HOMEMADE SAUSAGES WITH MINESTRONE VEGETABLES

3 METRES (9ft) OF
SAUSAGE SKINS,
SOAKED FOR HALF
AN HOUR
450g (1lb) PORK
SHOULDER
225g (8oz)
PORK BELLY
150ml (5fl oz) WATER
1 RED CHILLI,
DE-SEEDED AND
FINELY DICED
A SPLASH OF DRY
WHITE WINE

2 GOOD PINCHES OF
NUTMEG, FRESHLY
GROUND
5 PINCHES OF DRIED
MARJORAM
1 PINCH OF ALLSPICE
1 PINCH OF FRESHLY
GROUND CUMIN
1 LEVEL TEASPOON
PAPRIKA
SALT AND
FRESHLY GROUND
BLACK PEPPER

Ask the butcher to mince the meat coarsely for you, or do it very quickly in a blender. Mix all the ingredients in a bowl and – this is the secret – knead the mixture for 10 minutes. You can always wear a pair of rubber gloves if you want to minimise what Adam Robinson calls the 'creature from the swamp' factor.

Cut the sausage skins into 12 pieces, each one some 23cm (9in) long. Fill a piping bag and, using a plain round nozzle, pipe in the mixture. Leave about 6cm (2in) at each end so you can tie the ends of the sausages easily.

Let them rest for half an hour. Then prick them and fry very gently in olive oil for 20 minutes on a low heat.

FOR THE MINESTRONE VEGETABLES

2 ONIONS	SALT AND
2 LARGE CARROTS	FRESHLY GROUND
1 LARGE SWEDE	BLACK PEPPER
2 CELERY STALKS	600ml (1 PINT)
2 BAKING POTATOES	SIEVED TOMATOES
1 RED OR GREEN	(PASSATA)
CHILLI, SEEDED AND	¼ PACKET OF
CHOPPED	DRIED PASTA
2 GARLIC CLOVES	CHOPPED PARSLEY
	TO GARNISH

Dice all the vegetables into bits about 2cm (¾in) long.

Chop the garlic finely, and sweat the onions, garlic and celery for 5 minutes until transparent. Add the diced carrots, swede and potatoes, sweat for a further 5 minutes, and season with plenty of freshly ground pepper. Add the tomatoes and simmer until the vegetables are slightly harder than *al dente*.

Add the uncooked pasta, which will draw the liquid out of the dish. Then ladle on to a plate or bowl with the sausages on top and lots of chopped parsley to garnish.

TAGINE OF LAMB

1.4kg (3lb)	CHOPPED FRESH
SHOULDER OF LAMB	CORIANDER FOR
	GARNISHING

FOR THE MARINADE

1 BUNCH OF FRESH	1 ORANGE, ZESTED
CORIANDER	AND SQUEEZED
3 RED CHILLIES	1 SMALL PACKET
2 GARLIC CLOVES	SAFFRON POWDER
1 LEMON, ZESTED	1 TEASPOON PAPRIKA
AND SQUEEZED	

For the Sauce

50g (2oz) FLOUR	600ml (1 PINT)
1 ONION	SIEVED TOMATOES
2 GARLIC CLOVES	(PASSATA)
2 TABLESPOONS	1 LARGE TIN 800g
OLIVE OIL	(28oz) CHOPPED
	TOMATOES

For the Couscous

450g (1lb) EASY-	175g (6oz) CHICKEN
COOK COUSCOUS	LIVER, FRIED AND
2 TOMATOES, SEEDED	CHOPPED (OPTIONAL)
AND CHOPPED	1 TABLESPOON
3 SPRING ONIONS,	CHOPPED MINT
CHOPPED	2 TABLESPOONS
1/3 CUCUMBER,	OLIVE OIL
DICED	

Put all the ingredients for the marinade into a blender and let it run for 5 minutes.

Remove the skinny fat from the lamb and cut the meat into healthy chunks – about 3 chunks for each person. None of yer poncy cubes, OK? Then pour the marinade over the meat and leave overnight.

The following day, sprinkle a little flour over the marinade so that it's lightly coated. To make the sauce, sweat the onion and garlic with a little olive oil for a few minutes until transparent, then add the meat and fry gently for about 5 minutes until it has taken on colour. Add the passata and tomatoes and simmer gently for 1 hour and 20 minutes. Alternatively you can cook the whole thing in a heavy casserole.

For the couscous, follow the instructions on the packet. And then just before it is ready to serve, add all the chopped vegetables, the liver (if using), the mint and the olive oil and mix well.

FOR THE GARNISHES

BABAGANOUSH

2 AUBERGINES
1 TABLESPOON
OLIVE OIL
2 SLICES OF
WHITE BREAD

2 PINCHES GROUND
CUMIN
JUICE OF ½ LEMON

Rub the aubergines with olive oil and bake in the hottest possible oven for 20 minutes until they start to collapse. Then cut them in half, scoop out the flesh and put it in a blender with the bread, the cumin and the lemon juice.

CUCUMBER SALAD

1 CUCUMBER,
DE-SEEDED AND
CHOPPED
2 TABLESPOONS
CHOPPED MINT

1 GARLIC CLOVE,
FINELY CHOPPED
1 SMALL POT GREEK
YOGHURT

Mix.

And for the final garnish, roast six long red chillies whole – brushed with olive oil – in the oven at the same time as you cook the aubergines.

Serve the garnishes on a dish, separately from the lamb and the couscous. Sprinkle the lamb with chopped coriander.

RHUBARB CRUMBLE TART WITH GINGER CUSTARD

FOR THE SWEET PASTRY

250g (8oz) FLOUR
125g (4oz) BUTTER
1 LEVEL DESSERTSPOON
ICING SUGAR
ZEST OF ½ LEMON
1 EGG

FOR THE RHUBARB

450g (1lb) RHUBARB
50g (2oz) SUGAR
150ml (5fl oz) WATER

FOR THE CRUMBLE

175g (6oz) FLOUR
15g (½oz) BUTTER
50g (2oz) CASTER SUGAR
6 CRUSHED AMARETTI BISCUITS OR
4 CRUMBLED DIGESTIVES (BOTH OPTIONAL)

FOR THE GINGER CUSTARD

600ml (1 PINT) MILK
75g (3oz) SUGAR
50g (2oz) GRATED FRESH GINGER
1 BAY LEAF
4 EGG YOLKS

For the pastry: Rub together the flour and butter, then add the icing sugar, the lemon zest, the egg and a dribble of cold water until it holds together. The trick is to handle it as little as possible. Wrap it in clingfilm and chill for half an hour.

Preheat the oven to 220°C/425°F/gas 7.

Roll out and line a flan dish with a detachable base, making sure the pastry overlaps the top because it will shrink when baked blind. Line with clingfilm, cover with dried beans and bake blind in the preheated oven for 15 minutes. When you take it out of the oven, knock off any extra pastry around the edges.

Meanwhile, cut the rhubarb into 2.5cm (1in) pieces, add the sugar and water and simmer until tender.

For the crumble: Rub the flour and butter into breadcrumbs and mix in the sugar and amaretti biscuits.

Finally, pour the rhubarb on to the pastry, put the crumble on top, put back in the oven, and bake for 15–20 minutes.

For the custard: Bring the milk to the boil with half the sugar, the ginger and the bay leaf.

Meanwhile, whisk the egg yolks with the rest of the sugar. Strain the hot milk over the eggs, stirring all the while. Then put back on the stove and heat through very gently, stirring all the while, until it coats the back of a spoon. Remove from the heat and keep stirring until it cools down a little.

RICHARD CORRIGAN
SEARCY'S

Richard Corrigan is a Michelin-star-winning, deep-end, over-the-top, never-a-dull-moment, intensely charming and generous Oirish egomaniac who'd be more fun to work for than anyone else alive.

TURNIP SOUP WITH TOULOUSE SAUSAGES AND CHILLI

2 LEEKS, CHOPPED
1 ONION, CHOPPED
2 GARLIC CLOVES, CHOPPED
2 CELERY STALKS, CHOPPED
1 RED OR GREEN CHILLI, SEEDED AND CHOPPED
FRESH OR DRIED THYME
1 BAY LEAF

2 TABLESPOONS OLIVE OIL
900g (2lb) TURNIPS, PEELED AND CHOPPED
600ml (1 PINT) LIGHT CHICKEN STOCK
4 TOULOUSE SAUSAGES
2 TABLESPOONS CHOPPED FLAT-LEAF PARSLEY FOR GARNISH

Sweat the leeks, onion, garlic, celery, half the chilli, the thyme and the bay leaf in olive oil for a few minutes until the vegetables are soft and transparent. Add the turnips and cook for another couple of minutes or so until they're well coated with oil and have taken on the flavour of the other vegetables. Add the stock, bring to the boil, cover and simmer gently for 25 minutes. Remove the thyme and bay leaf, then liquidise and strain.

In the meantime, slice the Toulouse sausages and fry gently

with the other half of the chilli. When they're cooked, throw in the chopped parsley and add them to the soup.

IRISH STEW

1.2kg (2½lb) NECK OF LAMB	½ BAY LEAF
900g (2lb) POTATOES, PEELED AND SLICED	600ml (1 PINT) LAMB STOCK (MADE WITH LAMB BONES, ONIONS, CARROTS AND CELERY)
450g (1lb) CARROTS	
SALT AND FRESHLY GROUND BLACK PEPPER	
1 SPRIG OF FRESH THYME	

Remove the meat and the trimmings from the bone and cut into healthy chunks.

Preheat the oven to 150°C/300°F/gas 2.

Lay the meat and vegetables in layers in a deep, buttered casserole, seasoning each layer well, adding the thyme and bay leaf, and ending with potatoes on top.

Pour over the stock and cover first with a piece of buttered foil and then with the lid. Bake in the preheated oven for 2 hours, adding a little more stock if necessary. Serve with red cabbage salad.

RED CABBAGE SALAD

1 SMALL RED CABBAGE	VINAIGRETTE TO TASTE
SALT	

Shred the cabbage finely, then cover liberally with salt and leave for 6 hours. Wash, drain and toss in the vinaigrette.

Chocolate Sorbet with Orange and Tarragon Salad

Everyone who has seen this recipe pulls faces. But it comes from Fredy Girardet, one of the Most Famous Chefs in Europe and the owner of the Hôtel de Ville at Crissier outside Lausanne.

For the Sorbet

500ml (16fl oz) water
250g (9oz) sugar
250g (9oz) good quality
dark chocolate
zest of 1 orange

Bring the water and sugar to the boil to make a syrup, then take it off the heat and let it cool down until warm. Melt the chocolate in a bain-marie. Stir in the orange zest and add the syrup to the chocolate. They should both be at the same temperature. Then freeze.

For the Salad

7 oranges
1 tablespoon chopped
tarragon

Warm the juice of 1 orange, and infuse it with the tarragon.

Segment the other oranges, to which you add the tarragon-and-orange-juice infusion.

Serve a dollop of sorbet in the centre of the orange and tarragon salad.

GILLIAN ENTHOVEN
LE MESURIER

Old Street, on the edge of the City, is one of the ugliest streets in London – bleak, derelict and windswept. It's Stephen Poliakoff land. Long stretches got left behind by developers during the eighties. It's about as welcoming as the Cromwell Road. I've cycled along it virtually every day, twice a day, for the past ten years, and its only redeeming feature is a ruined church, St Marks, which is collapsing under the weight of sheer misery.

Until, that is, I walked into Le Mesurier. Outside are the lorries, the roundabout and a Kwik Save, a few battered newsagents and the fog of exhaust fumes. Inside, behind the Venetian blinds, Le Mesurier is all light and mirrors, with daffodils and white linen and wineglasses and original underground posters on the walls dating from the 1930s.

It's like coming across an immaculately cut linen jacket lying across a sewer. Since then, I've been phoning everyone I know who works in the City with an expense account, both of them, urging them to go there. Which is mad, of course, because Le Mesurier is a well-known secret. Businessmen have been taking their mistresses there for years and when it stopped serving meals in the evening actors' Equity almost called a strike.

During the sixties, Gillian Enthoven's husband was working as an architect in Sierra Leone. She found herself with time on her hands. They did a lot of entertaining and she became fascinated by cooking. Recipes were measured out, not in grams or fluid ounces, but in eggshells. 'Take half an eggshell of flour, four eggshells of milk,' that sort of thing.

When they returned to England, she had four children,

including twin daughters, and when they reached a certain age, somewhere between toddling and O-levels, she set off round the City cooking directors' lunches.

She runs Le Mesurier almost single-handed. She's the chef and proprietor, the dishwasher and accountant. ('I use an old-fashioned ledger. And these marvellous clear folders you line up, month by month, on a shelf. I hang the bills from hooks until I've paid them.')

Her husband designed the restaurant, and he has his architectural offices on the floor above. The flat above is occupied by a friend of one of their daughters from the rock group Black Dog, which provides the backing for Björk and much confusion for the postman. ('Something here for a black dog . . .')

I asked if her husband always eats in the restaurant. Popping downstairs for a quick salmon soufflé surely beats going out into Old Street for a sausage roll and a KitKat. But in fact he only eats there when he wants to chat up a prospective client. Otherwise he just nips downstairs to help with the washing up. ('Oh yes – he's *terribly* nice,' she says.) The Enthoven household – black dogs, twin daughters, dishwashing architects – is clearly an infinitely welcoming place. Not surprising that the moment people walk into Le Mesurier out of Old Street, they start to feel better.

BEETROOT AND SPINACH SALAD WITH HOT BACON, AND ORANGE AND CARAWAY DRESSING

6 RASHERS SMOKED
STREAKY BACON
2 TABLESPOONS
OLIVE OIL
1 GARLIC CLOVE,
PEELED AND
CRUSHED
1 TEASPOON SUGAR
1 TEASPOON
CARAWAY SEEDS
JUICE OF 1 ORANGE
SALT AND
FRESHLY GROUND
BLACK PEPPER
700g (1½lb) COOKED
BEETROOT, PEELED
AND DICED
175g (6oz) YOUNG
SPINACH LEAVES

Cut the bacon into 1cm (½in) pieces and fry in the oil until crisp. Remove from the pan and keep warm.

Add the garlic and sweat gently for a minute or so. Then add the sugar, caraway seeds and orange juice, with salt and pepper to taste. Cook for a couple of minutes, scraping any bits off the bottom of the pan and stirring them into the dressing.

Just before serving, tip the diced beetroot into the pan and shake it all about until well coated, but don't cook it any more.

Arrange the spinach leaves on 6 plates, divide the dressed beetroot between them and garnish with the bacon.

SALMON SOUFFLÉ

75g (3oz) GRUYÈRE
CHEESE, GRATED,
PLUS EXTRA FOR
DUSTING DISH
225g (8oz) SALMON
450ml (¾ PINT) MILK
6 SHALLOTS,
FINELY DICED
75g (3oz) BUTTER
75g (3oz) FLOUR
1½ TABLESPOONS
TOMATO PURÉE

1 (SCANT) TEASPOON
OREGANO OR
MARJORAM
SALT AND
FRESHLY
GROUND
BLACK PEPPER
5 EGG YOLKS
6 EGG WHITES

Butter a 1.7 litre (3 pint) soufflé dish and dust with a little of the grated cheese.

Poach the salmon for about 5 minutes in the simmering milk. Remove it and put to one side. Keep the milk.

Gently sweat the chopped shallots in the butter for a minute or so. Add the flour and cook gently for a further couple of minutes. Remove from the heat.

Bring the milk (in which you cooked the salmon) back to the boil, and beat it into the flour and shallots, along with the tomato purée, herbs and seasoning. Then beat in the egg yolks, one at a time, and then the salmon and most of the cheese, leaving just enough cheese to sprinkle on top.

Meanwhile, preheat the oven to 200°C/400°F/gas 6.

Beat the egg whites with a pinch of salt until they're stiff. Stir about a quarter of them into the soufflé mixture and fold in the rest.

Turn out the mixture into the soufflé dish and sprinkle with the rest of the cheese. Place in the centre of the preheated oven. Turn the heat down to 190°C/375°F gas 5 and bake for between 30 and 35 minutes.

PEPPERMINT PARFAIT

175g (6oz) SUGAR
250ml (8fl oz) WATER
3 EGG WHITES
300ml (10fl oz)
DOUBLE CREAM
4 DROPS OF PURE
PEPPERMINT OIL
(OR MUCH

MORE IF YOU'RE
USING CHEAPER
PEPPERMINT
ESSENCE)
A DROP OR TWO
OF RED FOOD
COLOURING

Heat the sugar and water gently in a heavy-bottomed saucepan until the sugar has dissolved. Then boil it hard for 5 minutes, keeping an eye on it. Don't let it darken. Put it to one side, keeping it warm.

Meanwhile, beat the egg whites until very stiff. Slowly pour in the sugar syrup in a thin trickle, beating all the while. Let it cool in the fridge.

In another bowl, whip the cream until stiff and add the peppermint oil and colouring. When the egg whites are cold, combine both mixtures. It should be pale pink. Pour into a container and freeze.

When it comes to serving, and in a perfect world, dribble a little crème de menthe over each portion and garnish with a sprig of mint.

DAVID EYRE
THE EAGLE

On the one hand, there's the traditional British pub. Warm, watery, headachy beer. Greasy, tasteless, overcooked stodge for food. Fetid carpeting. Pinball machines in one corner, slot machines in the other. A television up above.

Empty, the traditional pub has the smelly desolation of a deserted cinema. Full, it's about as much fun as travelling on the tube in the rush hour.

On the other hand, there's the Eagle. Next door to the *Guardian* and opposite the Quality Chop House on Farringdon Road. The floorboards are bare, the walls are pale custard yellow and the ceiling is laurel green. There are a dozen or so tables dotted round and a battered red leather sofa at one end. A counter runs the length of the room, piled high with plates, bowls, bread baskets and cutlery. The menu is chalked up on blackboards and the food is fresh, Mediterranean and generous. There's a wide variety of wines and little pots of espresso if you just want coffee.

It's run by David Eyre, an effortlessly groovy Mel Gibson figure in a baseball cap. Aside from running the Eagle and writing a regular cookery column, he was yet another chef who couldn't have been friendlier or more helpful if his life had depended on it.

CALDO VERDE

1 LARGE HEAD OF SPRING GREENS (ANY CABBAGE GREEN WILL DO)	150ml (5fl oz) OLIVE OIL
	SALT AND FRESHLY GROUND BLACK PEPPER
150g (5oz) CHORIZO SAUSAGE	4 LARGE POTATOES
1 LARGE ONION, CHOPPED	1 BAY LEAF
2 GARLIC CLOVES, CRUSHED	2 LITRES (3½ PINTS) WATER OR CHICKEN STOCK

Roll the dark green leaves of the greens as tightly as possible into cigars and shred, as finely as possible, with a very sharp knife. Only use the dark green leaves. The thinner they're shredded, the better.

Fry the chorizo sausage until almost crisp. Drain away the fat.

Gently sweat the onion and garlic in the olive oil, with salt and pepper, for a few minutes until transparent. Add the potatoes, peeled and finely diced. Cook for a further 5 minutes so they're all nicely coated in the oil, add water just to cover, and put in the bay leaf. Bring to the boil and simmer for 20 minutes until the potatoes are soft. Then mash the potatoes and add the rest of the water.

Bring the soup back to the boil, add the chorizo sausage and greens and heat through for 5 minutes. Check the seasoning and serve with an extra dribble of olive oil.

PAPPARDELLE PASTA WITH CHICKEN LIVERS

2 GARLIC CLOVES, BRUISED
50ml (2fl oz) OLIVE OIL
600g (1¼lb) CHICKEN LIVERS
1 WINEGLASS WHITE WINE
10 SAGE LEAVES
SALT AND FRESHLY GROUND BLACK PEPPER
450g (1lb) PAPPARDELLE PASTA
FRESHLY GRATED PARMESAN

Fry the garlic in the olive oil in a large, heavy frying pan. Just before the garlic turns brown, remove. All you're doing is flavouring the oil – for heaven's sake don't let the garlic burn.

Add the whole chicken livers, cleaned of any unattractive bits of attached green slime, to the hot oil ('the fat will splatter and jump up at you,' he says, 'but never mind') and fry for approximately 5 minutes until they're brown. Then pour in the wine and add the whole sage leaves, reduce the heat and let it all bubble away gently for 10 minutes or so – the livers should be just cooked and still slightly pink inside. Check the seasoning.

Mix it all up into the cooked pasta and scatter generously with freshly grated Parmesan.

LIME SYLLABUB

2 TABLESPOONS WHITE WINE
1 TABLESPOON BRANDY
2 LIMES (JUICE OF 2 AND ZEST OF 1)
25g (1oz) CASTER SUGAR
600ml (1 PINT) DOUBLE CREAM

Whisk together the wine, brandy, lime juice and zest and sugar

175

in a bowl until the sugar has dissolved. Then whisk in the cream until you have soft peaks.

Cover and chill, and serve with ratafia or amaretti biscuits, or sweet macaroons.

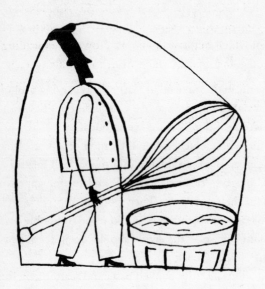

MATTHEW FANTHORPE
DELL' UGO

Matthew Fanthorpe's mother is Australian and her side of the family settled in California. His uncle has a seafood restaurant in San Francisco, and he would eventually like to open a restaurant on Cape Cod. All of which might go some way towards explaining why he's so easy-going and genial, which from my point of view was very fortunate. The first time I was due to see him, I managed to get the time wrong by some six hours. And the second time, the following day, I turned up half an hour early but in the wrong place – there are now two dell' Ugos. He didn't seem in the least put out: 'At least you weren't organising the Gulf War,' he said. 'Desert Storm would have started a month late.'

And it gets worse. He gave me a recipe for faggots, made with apples and mint and roasted in the oven. I cooked it that night. Prepared the meat, mixed up all the ingredients, wrapped them all up in the white lining of a lamb's stomach which was supposed to all-but-disappear in the cooking, and popped them in the oven. Heaven alone knows what I did to them, but whatever it was, it turned out to be profoundly disgusting. They tasted like balls of gristly, warm corned beef wrapped in a satanic fat. So we threw the whole thing away, opened the windows wide to let some in some fresh air, and ate scrambled eggs for supper instead.

I rang him up the following day and, again, he didn't seem in the least put out and was as genial as ever. 'Drop by whenever you feel like it. I'll give you another recipe. How about pig's trotters? No? Well, whatever . . . When is a good time for you?' he asked. 'Approximately.'

Warm Mussel Salad with Roast Onions and a Tomato Confit

2kg (4½ 1lb) MUSSELS	OLIVE OIL
3 BIG TOMATOES	450g (1lb) BABY ONIONS
ROCK SALT AND FRESHLY GROUND BLACK PEPPER	50g (2oz) BUTTER
	1 LETTUCE
	LEMON JUICE

Scrub the mussels, pulling out the hairy beards and discarding any that are broken. Put them into a big pot with 1cm (½in) of water and steam them open. Drain through a fine sieve, retaining the liquor. When they've cooled, remove the flesh from the mussels and throw away the shells. Then put the liquor into a saucepan or a frying pan, and boil away until it has reduced by some three-quarters. What you want to end up with is a very small quantity of concentrated liquid.

Meanwhile, cut each large tomato into 8 wedges, removing the seeds. Spread them on a baking tray, skin side up, sprinkle with rock salt and freshly ground black pepper, trickle with olive oil, cover with silver foil and put in a very low oven (70°C/160°F/gas ¼) for 2 hours. The end result is soft pieces of tomato, rich and concentrated in flavour and infused with the flavour of olive oil.

Peel the onions. (They're much easier to peel if you leave them in warm water for half an hour beforehand.) Melt the butter in a baking dish. Toss the onions in the butter and bake in the oven at 200°C/400°F/gas 6 for 15 minutes, until they're soft to the touch and golden brown.

To assemble: arrange a bed of lettuce on each plate – ideally rocket or lamb's lettuce. Warm the mussels through and mix with the baby onions. The mixture should be warm rather than hot –

you don't want to wilt the lettuce. Make a dressing with the mussel liquor, olive oil and lemon juice. Adjust the seasoning, coat the mussels and the onions and pour on to the lettuce, with the tomato confit on top.

It's fiendishly attractive.

A CASEROLE OF WILD RABBIT WITH CREAM AND TARRAGON

2 WILD RABBITS
SALT AND
FRESHLY GROUND
BLACK PEPPER
50g (2oz) BUTTER
1 ONION, FINELY
CHOPPED
2 GARLIC CLOVES,
CRUSHED

1 LEEK, FINELY
CHOPPED
2 LITRES (3½ PINTS)
DARK CHICKEN
STOCK (SEE BELOW)
1 BUNCH TARRAGON
1 SMALL CARTON
DOUBLE CREAM

Ask your friendly butcher to chop the rabbits into pieces for you. Season them with salt and pepper, and fry in butter for 5 minutes or so until the pieces are golden brown, to seal the meat. Remove and place in a heavy casserole.

In the same frying pan, sauté the onions, garlic and leek until they're soft and add them to the casserole. Deglaze the pan with a cup of stock (in other words, pour in a cup of stock and scrape around the bottom of the pan with a wooden spoon to make sure you get all the juicy bits out) and add to the casserole with the rest of the stock. Remove the leaves from the tarragon and reserve. Tie the stalks together and add to the casserole. Preheat the oven to 190°C/375°F/gas 5 and cook for 2 hours.

One minute before serving, remove the casserole from the oven and add the cream and the coarsely chopped tarragon leaves. Stir well and correct the seasoning.

179

Serve with a purée of celeriac.

Note: Brown chicken stock is exactly the same as ordinary chicken stock, except that the chicken bits and vegetables have been first roasted in a hot oven before they go into the stock.

CELERIAC PURÉE

1 HEAD OF CELERIAC
900g (2lb) STARCHY
POTATOES
50ml (2fl oz) MILK
125g (4oz) BUTTER

NUTMEG
SALT AND
FRESHLY GROUND
BLACK PEPPER

Peel the celeriac and potatoes and chop into 2.5cm (1in) cubes. Cover with salted cold water, bring to the boil and simmer for half an hour. Drain and mash. Heat the milk. Add the butter, the hot milk, a pinch of freshly grated nutmeg and correct the seasoning.

A STEAMED SHERRY AND RAISIN SPONGE

250g (8oz) BUTTER
250g (8oz) CASTER
SUGAR
250g (8oz) EGGS
(SEE BELOW)

250g (8oz) SEEDLESS
RAISINS, SOAKED
OVERNIGHT IN 50ml
(2fl oz) SHERRY
400g (14oz)
SELF-RAISING FLOUR

Cream the butter and sugar together in a food processor for between 2 and 3 minutes, and then whizz in the eggs a little at a time.

Put the mixture into a large bowl. Add the raisins and sherry. Then fold in the flour until it's fully absorbed, using a wooden or a plastic spatula so you don't knock all the air out.

Prepare a pudding bowl by buttering the sides and coating with flour. Pour in the mixture. Tie foil around the top of the basin. Place in a large saucepan with water half-way up the side of the bowl, pop the lid on and steam for 2½ hours, topping up the water from time to time. To test if it's cooked, stick in a skewer, a knitting needle or a horse syringe, and if it comes out dry, the sponge is ready.

Serve with crème anglaise.

Note: Crack the eggs into the bowl of a weighing scale until you reach 250g (8oz). The recipe calls for equal parts of butter, egg and sugar, and egg sizes vary.

MARY HEALEY

THE CHERRY ORCHARD

The Cherry Orchard is a vegetarian restaurant in the East End, run as a cooperative by five girls in their thirties who live and work together as Buddhists. The basic precepts by which they try to live their lives, expressed both negatively and positively, are:

- Abstinence from harming living beings. The practice of love and kindness.
- Abstinence from taking that which is not given. The practice of generosity.
- Abstinence from sexual misconduct. (Misconduct being exploitation rather than promiscuity.) The practice of simplicity and contentment.
- Abstinence from untruthful speech. The practice of honesty.
- Abstinence from intoxicants that cloud the mind. The practice of clarifying the mind.

They meditate together each morning before cycling to the restaurant, where they spend the day cheerfully serving large numbers of people delicious and inexpensive food.

TARRAGON AND RED PEPPER SOUP

2 MEDIUM ONIONS	1 BIG TIN
4 MEDIUM RED	(800g/28oz)
PEPPERS	TOMATOES.
1 TABLESPOON	½ TEASPOON DRIED
OLIVE OIL	TARRAGON
¼ TEASPOON	SALT AND
CAYENNE	FRESHLY GROUND
600ml (1 PINT)	BLACK PEPPER
VEGETABLE STOCK	YOGHURT TO
	GARNISH

Slice the onions and the red peppers and sauté them in olive oil for 10–15 minutes with the cayenne until they're soft and translucent.

Add the stock, tomatoes and tarragon and simmer for 20 minutes.

Blend, season, and serve with a dollop of yoghurt.

CREAM OF CAULIFLOWER SOUP WITH ALMONDS

2 MEDIUM ONIONS	1 SMALL
1 TABLESPOON	CAULIFLOWER
OLIVE OIL	SALT AND
PINCH OF CURRY	FRESHLY GROUND
POWDER	BLACK PEPPER
1.2 LITRES (2 PINTS)	50g (2oz) TOASTED,
VEGETABLE STOCK	FLAKED ALMONDS

Finely chop the onions and sauté them in olive oil with the curry powder. (Be very circumspect with the curry powder – the idea is that it should add a hint of something remote and unidentifiable, not turn the whole caboosh into a flaming vindaloo.)

Add the vegetable stock.

183

Roughly chop the entire cauliflower, except for the leaves, add to the pan, and simmer for 20 minutes. Blend, adjust the seasoning, and stir in the almonds.

CAULIFLOWER AND CASHEW PIE

1 MEDIUM
CAULIFLOWER
2–3 GRATED
CARROTS
600ml (1 PINT)
THICK BÉCHAMEL
SAUCE (MADE WITH
½ WINEGLASS
WHITE WINE AND

½ TEASPOON DRIED
TARRAGON)
125g (4oz) CASHEWS,
TOASTED
1 PACKET FILO
PASTRY
MELTED BUTTER

Remove the flowerets from the cauliflower and chop some of the stalk very finely. Add the carrots and the cauliflower to the béchamel, cook for 10 minutes, then add the cashews.

Meanwhile, preheat the oven to 200°C/400°F/gas 6 and line a buttered 23cm (9in) dish with 5 layers of filo pastry, brushing between each layer with melted butter. Bake for 5 minutes to a very pale golden brown.

Pour in the béchamel and vegetables, then place a lid on top made from another 5 layers of filo pastry, again brushing with melted butter between each layer. (The trick is to assemble the lid on a board by the side and then transfer it over in one piece, cutting it to size.)

Using the point of a knife, mark the pie crust into portions, making sure you don't cut right through it. Brush with melted butter and bake for a further 10–15 minutes. Serve with a green salad.

FRUIT SHORTCAKE

150g (6oz) BUTTER   75g (3oz) CASTER
150g (6oz) PLAIN   SUGAR
FLOUR (SIFTED)

Plus an assortment of whatever fruit is available and would look pretty: strawberries, kiwis, grapes, plums, slices of orange, banana, etc.

Melted jam or jelly to glaze.

Cream, yoghurt or crème fraîche to serve.

Preheat the oven to 200°C/400°F/gas 6.

Rub the butter and flour together until they resemble very fine breadcrumbs. Stir in the sugar.

Press the mixture hard to the thickness of 1cm (½in) on to the base of a tray, prick all over with a fork, and bake in the preheated oven for 15 minutes until pale golden brown.

Paint with melted jelly, then cover with an arrangement of peeled, sliced fruit. It depends what grabs your artistic fancy, but straight lines of fruit are attractive.

Finally, glaze with melted jelly and serve with cream, yoghurt or crème fraîche.

Fergus Henderson
St John

St John is an old smoke house in Smithfield, transformed into huge white rooms with high ceilings and stairs, specialising in inexpensive cuts of meat. Cow's ear lobe, that sort of thing. Fergus Henderson, the chef, trained as an architect and only switched to cooking when his buildings started to become an excuse to sit down and celebrate. ('Right. That's the Lloyds' building done. Bit worried about the pudding, though . . .')

Clearly there is a strong correlation between cooking and architecture. Mind you, there's a correlation between food and just about anything provided you stare at it long enough. But *especially* between food and buildings. It's to do with turning a recipe or a set of drawings into something three-dimensional, while at the same time thinking of all the other variables – weather conditions, the availability of ingredients and so on.

Henderson's first industrial cooking involved taking over a restaurant in Covent Garden at the weekend with some friends, sending out fliers and doing one-pot Sunday lunches for 200 people at a go. Le Creuset provided the pots, and Henderson and Co. would plonk a huge pot of cassoulet in the middle of a table of ten. It was a great success and the chef of the restaurant – an Olympic hop, skip and jumper – offered him a job. Apart from an interlude at a strange and ropy Notting Hill club, he's never looked back . . .

CHICKEN BROTH WITH WILD GARLIC

900g (2lb) CHICKEN WINGS OR 2 CHICKEN CARCASSES
2 CARROTS
2 ONIONS
2 LEEKS
2 CELERY STALKS
1 BAY LEAF
FRESH OR DRIED THYME
1 HEAD OF GARLIC, CUT ACROSS
1.2 LITRES (2 GENEROUS PINTS) WATER
SALT AND FRESHLY GROUND BLACK PEPPER
2 LEAVES OF WILD GARLIC, CHOPPED

Make the broth by throwing everything into a pot – except for the wild garlic – and letting it simmer gently for an hour or so.

Strain, season, and then just before serving, add the wild garlic. 'At first it might appear quite bland,' says Henderson, 'but the addition of the garlic at the end makes it all kind of happen.'

187

BOILED HAM WITH PARSLEY SAUCE

1.2kg (2½ lb) GREEN
UNSMOKED COLLAR
OF HAM, BONED AND
ROLLED

1 ONION, STUDDED
WITH 10 CLOVES
1 BAY LEAF
A FEW PEPPERCORNS
12 CARROTS

FOR THE PARSLEY SAUCE

A HEALTHY KNOB OF
BUTTER
2 TABLESPOONS
FLOUR
300ml (½ PINT) MILK
300ml (½ PINT)
LIQUID FROM
THE HAM

A LARGE BUNCH
OF PARSLEY, VERY
FINELY CHOPPED
SALT AND
FRESHLY GROUND
BLACK PEPPER

Cover the ham with water, add the onion and cloves, the bay leaf and peppercorns, bring to the boil and simmer very gently – with barely a murmur on the surface of the water – for 3 hours.

Half an hour before the ham is cooked, add the carrots. (Carrots don't need as much as half an hour in the normal course of events, but you're cooking this at a very gentle simmer.)

For the parsley sauce: Make a roux by melting the butter, stirring in the flour and cooking for a couple of minutes until it smells biscuity. Add the liquid – the milk and the broth from the ham – a little at a time, stirring all the while. Finally, add the parsley and adjust the seasoning.

Note: Henderson prefers to use the much-maligned curly British parsley for this. Funny chap old Fergus.

CARAGEEN MILK PUDDING

Useful recipe if you live in Ireland or the Outer Hebrides, where you can pick the carageen moss for naught. Otherwise you have to buy it at a premium from a health food shop.

1 HAPPY HANDFUL OF CARAGEEN	1 LEMON, BOTH ZEST AND JUICE
900ml (1½ PINTS) MILK	3 TABLESPOONS WHITE SUGAR

Carageen contains a kind of gelatine which will set the pudding. Simmer all the ingredients together until the mixture coats the back of a spoon. Strain it into pudding basins, allow to set and serve with a dollop of some delicious homemade jam you happen to have in the cupboard.

(Henderson describes it as 'rather like a junket with a strange, subliminal taste. Not ooomphy, but peculiar and delicious.')

TONY HOWORTH
LE CAFÉ DU JARDIN

Tony Howorth is a gentle giant with craggy features and huge sculptor's hands. When we shook hands, mine seemed to disappear completely. It's easier to imagine him hammering away at an enormous piece of marble in a quarry in Carrara than rolling out pastry in a kitchen.

But again, there's no mistaking the fact that he's a chef. Like so many of the chefs I spoke to, cooking is something he thinks about and talks about and carries around with him as part of his mental baggage all day long. He recently came back from six months in Australia and Los Angeles, where he walked into restaurants and asked to cook in their kitchens for nothing. 'You can't stand still. You've got to be constantly on the look-out for ideas,' he says. His enthusiasm for innovation and the friendliness of his manner were unwittingly encouraged by his training in France, where the chef chose the menu each day by consulting a bible of classic dishes, ignoring whatever might be in season and contemptuous of any deviation – a rigid fundamentalism applied to food. 'I'm forty-five now. I was nineteen then. I still remember it as the worst time of my life. The only thing I learned there was how not to treat foreigners.' He stuck it out for the sake of the reference, which began: 'Anthony Howorth has received the benefit of working in our restaurant . . .'

AVOCADO TARTARE

50g (2oz) BROCCOLI	SALT AND
50g (2oz)	FRESHLY GROUND
CAULIFLOWER	BLACK PEPPER
50g (2oz) FRENCH	JUICE OF 1 LEMON
BEANS	175g (6oz) CRÈME
1 AVOCADO	FRAÎCHE
4 TOMATOES,	1 TEASPOON
SKINNED AND	GRAIN OR HERB
SEEDED	MUSTARD

Peel the stems of the broccoli with a potato peeler so you don't waste any. Broccoli stalk is not unlike asparagus, so it would be a pity to waste it.

Blanch the broccoli, the cauliflower and the French beans in boiling salted water till they're cooked *al dente*, then drain and refresh under the cold tap.

Keep back 6 thin slices of avocado and tomato each for decoration, then dice all the vegetables into tiny pieces. Season, and mix with the lemon juice, crème fraîche and mustard.

Rub the inside of a cup with oil, then line with clingfilm. The oil helps the clingfilm to stick. Divide the vegetables into 6 portions. Put each portion into the cup and turn on to a plate, and garnish with the petals of avocado and tomato.

Note: There are ways of keeping tomatoes and avocados looking fresh. Avocados you can blanch in boiling water in their skins for a minute to stop them discolouring. Or dip the avocado slices in water with a Camden tablet dissolved in it – Camden tablets being the things you use to sterilise bottles in wine-making. (I asked Tony Howorth if Camden tablets killed the vitamins in the avocado, and he said: 'If you have to get 250 of these ready to serve in the half-hour or so when the theatres close, that's not a question I ever really asked myself.') And tomatoes, skinned and pipped and dried off between pieces of kitchen paper, will keep for up to 4 days in the fridge.

TOMATO GALETTE

350g (12oz) PUFF PASTRY	6 DESSERTSPOONS OLIVE OIL
125g (4oz) SUN-DRIED TOMATOES IN OIL, PURÉED	1 BUNCH OF BASIL SALT (IDEALLY, SEA SALT) AND
12 TOMATOES, SKINNED	FRESHLY GROUND BLACK PEPPER

Preheat the oven to 200°C/400°F/gas 6.

Roll out the puff pastry as thin as card (a pasta machine is perfect for this if you're lucky enough to have one) and cut into 15cm (6in) rounds.

Lay the pastry between 2 pieces of lightly oiled greaseproof paper, and then put the greaseproof paper between 2 baking sheets. (In other words, you have a sandwich consisting of baking sheet on top, then paper underneath, then the pastry, then another layer of paper and a baking sheet underneath that. I seem to be describing it in a very long-winded manner, but in fact it's pretty straightforward: pastry between 2 sheets of paper between 2 baking trays.)

Cook in the preheated oven for 15 minutes. You can always lift up the baking sheet to see if it's cooked. The pastry will come out like thin, brittle biscuit.

Spread the base of the biscuits with the puréed sun-dried tomatoes. Slice the skinned tomatoes, and arrange – overlapping – on top.

Warm through in the oven, then drizzle with the olive oil and sprinkle with chopped basil, sea salt and freshly ground pepper.

THINLY-SLICED ('WE'LL-THINK-OF-A-NAME-LATER') SALMON

4 CELERY STALKS	2 TABLESPOONS
4 CARROTS	OLIVE OIL)
2 LEEKS	700g (1½)
1 RED PEPPER	SALMON
1 GREEN PEPPER	250g (9oz)
2 MEDIUM ONIONS	FRESHLY MADE
2 GARLIC CLOVES	MAYONNAISE
4 TABLESPOONS	WITH BASIL
OLIVE OIL (OR 2	1 BAY LEAF
TABLESPOONS CORN	SEA SALT
OIL AND	BASIL LEAVES

Cut the celery, carrots, leeks and peppers into julienne strips – little strips of vegetables the thickness of a fat hair. It's a very time-consuming process, but restful if you settle down to it with the radio on.

Chop the onions and slice the garlic finely. Put all the vegetables in a saucepan with the oil, bay leaf and sea salt to taste and bring up the heat. You don't fry the vegetables, but it's a little more than simply heating them through. Then take off the heat and strain the vegetables, retaining the oil.

Carve the raw salmon very finely, as if you were slicing smoked salmon. Or, perhaps more realistically, be very nice to your fishmonger and ask him to do it for you.

Divide the vegetables between 6 plates. Cover each plate with the sliced salmon and brush lightly with the oil from the vegetables. Then flash the plates under a grill just so that the salmon turns opaque. Don't cook it.

Serve with basil mayonnaise, sprinkle with a little more salt, and garnish with basil leaves.

BANANAS EN PAPILLOTE

6 BANANAS	1 SHOT OF RUM
350g (12oz)	BUTTER FOR
CHOCOLATE	GREASING
175g (6oz)	THE PAPER
DEMERARA SUGAR	1 EGG WHITE
175ml (6fl oz)	125ml (4fl oz)
DOUBLE CREAM	CORN OIL

Cut the bananas in half lengthways, and coat completely in melted chocolate. While still moist, sprinkle with demerara sugar and allow to set.

Whip the cream and rum together.

Preheat the oven to 200°C/400°F/gas 6.

Take 6 sheets of greaseproof paper, 25 x 25cm (10 x 10in) each. Butter a square in the centre of each sheet, and brush the rest of the paper outside the buttered square with the egg white.

Lay each banana on a greased square, put some cream and rum on top, then fold up into parcels. The easiest way to do this is to take two sides of the paper and bring together above the bananas. Then fold the edge over once, then over once again, and finally fold the edge back on itself like a French seam. The egg white seals the edges.

Brush the sides of the bag with oil. Heat a little oil in a frying pan and dip the bags in the oil for about 10 seconds to get them started. It puffs up the bag. Then place in the preheated oven for 10 minutes.

GAIL KOERBER AND MARK NATHAN
THE MUSEUM STREET CAFÉ

The Museum Street Café opposite the British Museum is small, clean and simple: polished pine tables and absolutely no smoking. Don't even think about smoking – both Gail Koerber and Mark Nathan are committed drinkers of carrot juice. The menu is chalked up on a blackboard. The bread is baked on the premises every day. There's a charcoal grill. The ingredients are fresh, the prices reasonable, the place busy.

When I spoke to Gail on the phone, she agreed to see me, but only with a lot of pleading on my part and considerable reluctance on hers. She wasn't there when I arrived, but Mark was sitting at one of the tables. He had the petulant look of a slightly aggrieved hairdresser, surrounded by a pile of bills and invoices, a portable phone, an unopened copy of the *Independent* and a half-drunk glass of carrot juice. To all intents and purposes, he was wearing an enormous 'Do Not Disturb' sign round his neck.

Gail walked in a few minutes later. She has short dark hair straight out of *No No Nanette*. She gave me the sort of pursed-lip look that a Jehovah's Witness would be very familiar with, a blend of cross, blank and wary. 'Have you started yet?' she asked Mark.

'No, I was waiting for you.'

Her lips became even more pursed. He buried himself even deeper in his papers.

'Well, I've got to do the bread,' she said and headed towards the kitchen at the back.

In desperation, I asked if they'd like to look at some of the recipes that I'd got so far from other chefs, which seemed to help. They unthawed a little while they were reading, and even if we didn't end up on terms of cheerful intimacy, at least we had a pleasant enough conversation about mashed potato. I began to feel slightly less like a Jehovah's Witness and slightly more like an insurance salesman who'd been offered a cup of tea, even if it was offered in an I-suppose-you-might-as-well-come-in sort of way. Finally she said, 'Look, we really haven't had time to think about this properly. Could you come back later on and we'll have had time to sort something out?'

A week later I came back and there they were, sitting at the same table. The papers and the portable phone were still there, only this time there were major differences. There was no copy of the *Independent*. There were two half-drunk glasses of carrot juice instead of just the one. And they were very, very friendly.

FISH CHOWDER

FOR THE STOCK

1.4kg (3lb)	1.7 LITRES (3 PINTS)
FISH BONES	COLD WATER
1 LEEK	6 WHITE
2 CHOPPED ONIONS	PEPPERCORNS
2 CHOPPED CARROTS	BIG PINCH OF FRESH
1 CELERY STALK,	OR DRIED THYME
FINELY CHOPPED	1 BAY LEAF
A FEW PARSLEY	
STALKS	

FOR THE CHOWDER

125g (4oz) SMOKED, STREAKY BACON
1 TABLESPOON OLIVE OIL
1 ONION, CHOPPED
3 CELERY STALKS, FINELY DICED
1 LARGE LEEK, WASHED AND DICED
2 CHOPPED CARROTS
1 BAY LEAF
1 LARGE DICED POTATO

150ml (5fl oz) DOUBLE CREAM (OPTIONAL) OR MILK
450g (1lb) WHITE FISH FILLET (WHATEVER IS FRESH AND CHEAP)
PINCH OF CAYENNE
SALT AND FRESHLY GROUND BLACK PEPPER

To make the stock, put all the ingredients in a saucepan and bring slowly to the boil. Simmer for 20 minutes and strain.

Dice the bacon and fry in olive oil in a large saucepan until crisp. Add the chopped onion, celery, leek and carrots, and sweat until soft. Add the stock and bay leaf, and simmer for 20 minutes. Add the potato and simmer for a further 10 minutes.

Stir in the cream. Finally, add the fish and cook for 2 minutes. Add a pinch of cayenne and correct the seasoning.

197

GRILLED CHICKEN WITH PESTO

6 PORTIONS BONED
CHICKEN
½ WINEGLASS
WHITE WINE

3 TABLESPOONS
OLIVE OIL
FRESHLY GROUND
BLACK PEPPER

FOR THE PESTO

A SMALL HANDFUL
OF ALMONDS OR
PINE-NUTS
½ GARLIC CLOVE
4 TABLESPOONS
FRESHLY GRATED
PARMESAN CHEESE

A SMALL BUNCH OF
BASIL LEAVES
125ml (4fl oz)
OLIVE OIL

Marinate the chicken in a shallow dish with the white wine, olive oil and pepper for a couple of hours.

To make the pesto, toast the nuts in a medium oven (200°C/400°F/gas 6) for between 5 and 8 minutes. Either use a mortar and pestle, or put the nuts in a processor with the garlic, Parmesan and basil, and add the oil. Whizz it as little as possible – the pesto should resemble a rough paste.

Meanwhile, sprinkle the chicken pieces with salt and put under a very hot grill for 5 minutes each side, starting with the skin side down.

Serve with the pesto on top of the chicken – so that the heat from the chicken releases the scent of the basil and garlic – and a salad on the side.

INDIVIDUAL CHOCOLATE BREAD-AND-BUTTER PUDDINGS

2 CUPS BREAD CUBES	6 EGG YOLKS
4 TABLESPOONS BUTTER	ZEST OF ORANGE
250ml (8fl oz) MILK	125g (4oz) PLAIN CHOCOLATE
250ml (8fl oz) DOUBLE CREAM	3 TABLESPOONS SULTANAS
4 TABLESPOONS SUGAR	

Preheat the oven to 160°C/325°F/gas 3.

Sauté the bread cubes in butter until golden. Divide them between 6 ramekin dishes. Scald the milk and cream, stir in the sugar, and whisk into the egg yolks. Add the orange zest and the melted chocolate. Divide the sultanas evenly among the ramekins.

Let them sit for 5 minutes, and then put them in a baking dish with boiling water coming half-way up the sides and bake in the preheated oven for half an hour. Serve warm.

Laszlo Holecz
THE GAY HUSSAR

The food at the Gay Hussar is as hearty and unpretentious as you can get. Year after year, trenchermen have been tucking into vast portions of roast duck and red cabbage, followed by plates of crêpes and strudel, knocking back the Tokai and promising their loved ones that tomorrow they'll go on a diet.

Laszlo Holecz left Hungary in 1956, aged seventeen, in the immediate aftermath of the revolution, and he's been cooking at the Gay Hussar for almost twenty years. He was a total joy to meet. At four-thirty in the afternoon, the kitchen was all polished and peaceful. He was relaxed and welcoming. The recipes he produced were straightforward and delicious and inexpensive. His apple strudel, aside from being something very wonderful to eat, can be effortlessly cooked even by those of us who shouldn't normally be allowed anywhere near pastry.

Sadly, while I was there, the horse he'd backed at Aintree came in a close second. But then life isn't fair.

HUNGARIAN GREEN BEAN SOUP

1.4kg (3 lb) FRESH
GREEN BEANS
(RUNNER BEANS,
KENYAN BEANS . . .
WHATEVER)
1.7 litres (3 PINTS)
CHICKEN STOCK
½ ONION, FINELY
CHOPPED
SALT AND
FRESHLY GROUND
BLACK PEPPER

90ml (3fl oz)
VEGETABLE OIL
125g (4oz)
PLAIN FLOUR
1 GARLIC CLOVE,
CRUSHED
A PINCH OF PAPRIKA
600ml (1 PINT) MILK
2 TABLESPOONS
WHITE WINE
VINEGAR
A SPLASH OF CREAM

Slice the beans into 2.5cm (1in) long pieces. Add to the chicken stock along with the finely chopped onion; season with salt and pepper and bring to the boil. Simmer for 10 minutes.

Make a roux by heating the oil, gradually stirring in the flour and cooking until golden brown. Then remove from the heat, add the crushed garlic clove and a pinch of paprika, and whisk in the cold milk.

Add this to the beans and the chicken stock, along with 2 tablespoons of white wine vinegar and a dash of cream. Bring to the boil and serve with crusty bread.

MAGYAR MEATBALLS AND SAVOY CABBAGE

FOR THE MEATBALLS

2 ONIONS, CHOPPED	50g (2oz) SALT
5 TABLESPOONS VEGETABLE OIL (2 TABLESPOONS FOR FRYING THE ONIONS, 3 FOR COOKING THE MEATBALLS)	25g (1oz) WHITE PEPPER
	25g (1oz) FRESHLY GROUND BLACK PEPPER
	1 TABLESPOON FRESH PARSLEY
700g (1½lb) LEAN BELLY OF PORK, MINCED	1 TEASPOON MARJORAM (DRIED)
3 WHITE BREAD ROLLS	2 EGGS

Preheat the oven to 180°C/350°F/gas 4.

Fry the onions in a couple of tablespoons of vegetable oil until they're soft. Let them cool down and then add them to the minced pork, either in a bowl or a processor.

Soak the rolls in lukewarm water, then squeeze them out and chop them up. Add them to the meat, along with all the rest of the ingredients, except for the oil.

Shape the mixture into balls the size of large eggs. Cover the base of a roasting tray with 3 tablespoons of oil, put in the meatballs and surround with 150ml (5fl oz) of water to prevent the meat drying out while it's being cooked.

Bake in the preheated oven for 45 minutes.

FOR THE CABBAGE

3 POTATOES	125g (4oz)
1 SAVOY CABBAGE	PLAIN FLOUR
SALT AND WHITE	1 GARLIC CLOVE,
PEPPER	CRUSHED
90ml (3fl oz)	A PINCH OF PAPRIKA
VEGETABLE OIL	

Peel and dice the potatoes. Shred the cabbage, discarding the hard white stem. Add water to cover, season with salt and pepper, bring to the boil and simmer for 10 minutes.

Meanwhile, make a roux by heating the oil and stirring in the flour, stirring to get rid of any lumps. When the roux is golden brown, remove from the heat, add the crushed garlic and paprika. Stir it into the cabbage, bring to the boil and serve.

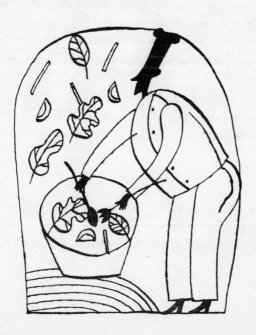

APPLE STRUDEL

400g (14oz) FROZEN FILO PASTRY, UNTHAWED
3 HANDFULS OF FRESH BREADCRUMBS
1.4kg (3lb) COOKING APPLES, PEELED AND GRATED
1 HANDFUL OF CHOPPED WALNUTS
50g (2oz) SULTANAS
125g (4oz) CASTER SUGAR
1 TEASPOON GROUND CINNAMON
VEGETABLE OIL

Preheat the oven to 180°C/350°F/gas 4.

Put a couple of damp tea-towels on the kitchen table.

Then lay the filo pastry on top of the tea-towels so that one sheet overlaps the other by an inch or so. Brush the overlapping edges with egg white to glue them together. Depending on the size of the sheets of pastry, the strudel can be laid either one or two sheets wide and about four sheets long.

Scatter the breadcrumbs three-quarters the length of the pastry, followed by the grated apple, the walnuts, the sultanas, the sugar and the cinnamon.

Then, using the tea-towel, roll it up. Lay it on an oiled baking tray and bake in the preheated oven for 10–15 minutes. Serve with cream or ice cream.

GARY PAVITT
CHARCO'S

Once upon a time, people wore flared trousers and the King's Road swung. These days, if you want to direct someone to Charco's, you tell them it's down the King's Road directly opposite Safeway.

I arrived there in a flurry of snow with a streaming cold in early March. Both entrances to the restaurant had signs above the door saying 'These premises are fully air-conditioned.'

Gary Pavitt, the chef, walked straight out of a Mike Leigh film. He's painfully thin, with the manner of someone who's smoked something the Metropolitan Police Commissioner wouldn't want to share. There was a Frank Sinatra album playing in the background and he'd softly hum and sing his way along with it during the pauses. And there were many, many pauses. But the music he was humming didn't appear to resemble the songs being played at the time, so the effect was strangely disconcerting. But it's not as if I made life any easier for him. I sat there, streaming with cold and noisily dying while my brain shut down completely. So while he peered into the middle-distance, chain-smoking Camels, I sneezed and spluttered and made all manner of bright suggestions. Things like: 'What about something with . . . those round things . . . Eggs. Something with eggs?' It was hardly the high table at Mensa.

POACHED EGGS WITH ENDIVE, CREAM AND BACON

6 EGGS
3 ENDIVES
1 TABLESPOON
WHITE WINE
VINEGAR
6 SLICES OF BACON
25g (1oz) BUTTER

150ml (5fl oz)
DOUBLE CREAM
2 TEASPOONS DIJON
MUSTARD
A PINCH OF SUGAR
A SPRIG OF
TARRAGON
(OPTIONAL)

Boil the endives, whole, in water with the vinegar for 10 minutes. Drain, allow to cool, and slice.

Grill the bacon, then cut it into pieces and put to one side.

Melt the butter in a frying pan and sweat the sliced endive for 5 minutes. Add the cream, mustard, sugar and tarragon, bring to the boil and reduce the sauce to a creamy consistency.

Pour the endive mixture on to 6 plates, place a poached egg on top of each, and garnish with the bacon.

Serve with croûtes, made by slicing pieces of French bread, rubbing them with garlic and drizzling with olive oil, and baking in the oven until golden.

SPICED MACKEREL WITH CRÉOSA SAUCE, AND SPINACH WITH SESAME SEEDS

6 SMALL MACKEREL,
OR 3 LARGE
MACKEREL, CUT
IN HALF
900g (2lb) SPINACH
BUTTER
SALT AND PEPPER

1 TABLESPOON
SESAME SEEDS,
ROASTED IN A DRY
FRYING PAN
1 TEASPOON
SESAME OIL

FOR THE MARINADE

1cm (½in) ROOT
GINGER, PEELED AND
CHOPPED
2 GARLIC CLOVES,
CHOPPED
½ TEASPOON
TURMERIC
½ TEASPOON
CAYENNE PEPPER

½ TABLESPOON
GROUND
CORIANDER
½ TABLESPOON
CHOPPED FRESH
CORIANDER
JUICE OF ½ LEMON

FOR THE SAUCE

3 SHALLOTS, CHOPPED (OR ½ SMALL ONION)
1 LARGE TOMATO, SKINNED AND PIPPED
½ CUCUMBER, PEELED, SEEDED AND DICED
½ RED PEPPER, ROASTED AND DICED (SEE BELOW)
6 SMALL GHERKINS, DICED
1 TABLESPOON CAPERS, DICED
A HANDFUL OF CHOPPED PARSLEY
100ml (3½fl oz) OLIVE OIL
1½ TABLESPOONS WHITE WINE VINEGAR
2 TABLESPOONS DIJON MUSTARD
SALT AND FRESHLY GROUND BLACK PEPPER

Mix all the marinade ingredients to a paste. Slash the skin of the mackerel and rub the marinade over the fish, leaving it for a minimum of 2 hours. Grill the fish for 8–10 minutes on each side.

Meanwhile, blanch the spinach in boiling water. Plunge it in and out, then refresh under cold water. Re-heat in a pan with a knob of butter, salt and pepper, a tablespoon of roasted sesame seeds (which you roast in a dry frying pan) and a teaspoon of sesame oil.

Stir together all the sauce ingredients. Serve the fish with the sauce on one side and the spinach on the other, garnished with fresh coriander.

Note: The easiest way to skin peppers is to hold them over a flame with a pair of tongs and then put them in a sealed bag to sweat. Then the skin more or less drops off.

RHUBARB AND GINGER PARFAIT

450g (1lb) RHUBARB
2 ORANGES
325g (11oz) CASTER SUGAR
250ml (8fl oz) MILK
1 TEASPOON VANILLA ESSENCE
6 EGG YOLKS
350ml (12fl oz) DOUBLE CREAM

2 EGG WHITES
3 BALLS OF STEM GINGER (THE STUFF IN A BOTTLE), GRATED
1 TABLESPOON GINGER SYRUP
1 TEASPOON ARROWROOT

Slice the rhubarb into 2.5cm (1in) pieces, and put them in a roasting tin with the zest of 1 orange, the juice of 2 oranges and 125g (4oz) caster sugar. Cook in the oven for 20 minutes at 190°C/375°F/gas 5. Cool and strain, reserving the liquid. Liquidise the rhubarb.

To make the parfait, bring the milk and the vanilla to the boil. Whisk the egg yolks with the rest of the sugar. Pour the boiling hot milk on to the yolks a little at a time, stirring all the while. Return the mixture to the pan, stirring continuously, until it thickens and coats the back of the spoon. Cool.

Whip the double cream to a thick slop – the consistency of yoghurt.

Separately, whip the egg whites in a similar fashion to the eggs. In other words, not completely stiff. Into hills that fall over, sort of thing.

Chop or grate the ginger, then fold all the ingredients together – the egg white, the cream, the rhubarb, the custard, the ginger and the ginger syrup.

Pour into a terrine lined with clingfilm, and freeze overnight.

To make a sauce, bring to the boil the liquor that was strained from the rhubarb, and then add a teaspoon of arrowroot mixed with a little cold water to thicken. Allow to cool, and serve with the parfait.

209

David Philpott
Quincy's

Nobody ever believes they've got their lives sorted out except for one or two people who clearly haven't.

I met David Philpott at home in Finchley, where he lives with his wife and two small children and lots of shelves. I've always admired people with shelves. Everything in his house was freshly painted and put away and and polished and clean. Outside the kitchen was a lawn that was lushly lawn-like. It was a sunny morning and he made a big pot of fresh coffee. His son pottered in, fell over and pottered out again.

When the phone rang, Philpott answered it with the sort of effortless niceness that comes from a lifetime of being nice. Someone else came to the door and exactly the same thing happened again. He is gentle and modest and unassuming and softly spoken. He's been at Quincy's now for the past five years which, because it's only open in the evenings, means he can spend a lot of the day with his family.

A pretty sorted-out sort of life, I'd say.

Bucatini Pasta with Mussels, Lemon and Chilli Pepper

900g (2lb) MUSSELS	3 TABLESPOONS
1 LEMON	OLIVE OIL
½ ONION, FINELY	2 TABLESPOONS
CHOPPED	CHOPPED PARSLEY
300g (10oz)	1 GARLIC CLOVE,
BUCATINI PASTA	FINELY CHOPPED
	1 HOT RED CHILLI

210

Clean the mussels, removing their hairy beards and throwing away any that are cracked. Put them in a big pot with the lemon juice and the chopped onion and steam them open.

Remove the mussels from the heat and discard half of each shell – keep the half of the shell each mussel is attached to. Reduce the mussel liquor.

Cook and drain the pasta. Dress it with the oil, parsley, garlic, chilli, lemon zest and the reduced mussel liquor.

TURKEY LEGS COOKED LIKE OSSO-BUCCO, WITH SOFT POLENTA AND BRAISED CELERY

2 TURKEY LEGS	1 GARLIC CLOVE
SALT AND	2 WINEGLASSES
FRESHLY GROUND	CHICKEN STOCK (OR
BLACK PEPPER	WATER)
1 TABLESPOON	1 WINEGLASS
FLOUR	WHITE WINE
3 TABLESPOONS	1 CARROT
CORN OIL	1 TIN TOMATOES
½ ONION	(400g/14oz)

Saw each turkey leg into three across the bone. You don't need a chain-saw for this – the bone is very soft. A Kitchen Devil would do the trick, anything with a serrated edge.

Toss the turkey slices in seasoned flour and fry for a few minutes in oil to seal them. Remove the turkey, then add the chopped onion and cook until it's soft. Add the chopped garlic and cook for 30 seconds, then the stock, the wine and the roughly chopped carrots and tomatoes.

Return the turkey to the pan. There should be enough liquid to cover. If there isn't, add more stock. Cover with greaseproof

211

paper directly on top, so that the paper is sitting on the turkey. Then put a lid on top of the whole thing and cook in a very slow oven (120°C/250°F/gas ½) for 2 hours.

FOR THE CELERY

1 LARGE BUNCH OF CELERY WITH LEAVES	1 CARROT, FINELY DICED
2 RASHERS OF BACON	

Cut a large bunch of celery into 6 lengthways and put it in a dish with the diced carrot and the raw bacon. Cover with foil and cook very gently for 1½ hours, or until tender.

FOR THE POLENTA

1 PACKET INSTANT POLENTA
(375g/13oz)
HEALTHY KNOB OF BUTTER
2 TABLESPOONS OLIVE OIL

Follow the instructions on the packet, but instead of the 1.5 litres (2½ pints) of water they tell you to use, use 2 litres (3½ pints) to get the right degree of sloppiness. Just before serving, whisk in a knob of butter and the olive oil.

APPLE DUMPLINGS WITH CRÈME FRAÎCHE

These aren't, of course, dumplings. More like apples wrapped in pastry, but never mind. Call them what you will, they taste lovely.

200g (7oz) FLOUR	50g (2oz) DRIED
100g (3½oz)	FRUIT
BUTTER	EGG-YOLK-AND-
50g (2oz) SUGAR	WATER WASH
1 EGG	CINNAMON AND
6 APPLES (COXES,	ICING SUGAR
WHATEVER)	TO DUST

To make the pastry, mix the flour, butter, sugar and egg in a whizzer. If the pastry is too crumbly, add a tablespoon of milk. Then wrap it in clingfilm and let it rest in the fridge for half an hour.

Peel and core the apples. Stuff them with the dried fruit.

Roll out the pastry and cut it into circles. Plonk each apple in the centre of a circle of pastry, folding the pastry upwards. Then turn each apple upside down so that the untidy joins are underneath.

Preheat the oven to 200°C/400°F/gas 6. Brush the pastry with the egg-yolk-and-water mix and bake the apples in the preheated oven for 20 minutes until golden. Dust with icing sugar and cinnamon, and serve with a dollop of crème fraîche. Or single cream, double cream, ice cream or Greek yoghurt.

Amanda Pritchett
The Lansdowne

The Lansdowne on Primrose Hill has the same sort of feel as the Eagle on Farringdon Road, which isn't altogether surprising since Amanda Pritchett worked there before setting up on her own. It's a devastatingly effective formula, the kind of thing that one wishes would be repeated over and over again all over England to breathe new life into England's tired pub scene. Basically, you take a great big old pub, keep whatever features are worth keeping and gut the rest. Then you splash a coat of paint around, pull up the carpets and sand down the floors. Fill the place with a medley of battered old sofas, tables and chairs, and light a fire in the corner. The Lansdowne may not actually have a fire – I can't remember – but it's so overflowing with good cheer that a fire is understood. There are blackboards hither and thither announcing an extensive selection of wine. And they serve food to boast about. Pub food as pub food never was. Out go lukewarm and congealed slabs of decomposing shepherd's pie full of grease and gristle under conical sun lamps. In come homemade sausages and piles of fresh salad with spinach and rocket.

Incidentally, there's stuff you should know about Amanda Pritchett for the next time you play trivial pursuit. In no particular order:

- She did a stint at Simply Nico.
- She has a bad back from falling off a horse.
- Like David Gower, she was very good at maths at school.

SOUSED MACKEREL

3 MACKEREL	8 WHOLE
300ml (½ PINT)	PEPPERCORNS
WHITE WINE	2 BAY LEAVES
VINEGAR	2.5cm (1in) STICK
3 CHOPPED	CINNAMON
SHALLOTS	SALT AND
FRESH DILL, CHIVES,	FRESHLY GROUND
PARSLEY (ANY	BLACK PEPPER
OR ALL)	

Preheat the oven to 160°C/325°F/gas 3.

Fillet the mackerel. Place the fillets in an ovenproof dish and cover with vinegar and water (3 parts vinegar to 1 part water). Add the shallots and all the herbs and spices. Bake for 40 minutes in the preheated oven, and allow to cool.

Serve cold with sour cream, wholemeal toast and a happy sprinkling of chives.

CORIANDER SOUP

3 MEDIUM ONIONS	1.7 litres (3 PINTS)
6 GARLIC CLOVES	CHICKEN STOCK OR
75ml (2½fl oz)	WATER
OLIVE OIL	SALT AND
4 MEDIUM	FRESHLY GROUND
POTATOES, PEELED	BLACK PEPPER
AND SLICED	1 BUNCH OF
	CORIANDER,
	ROUGHLY CHOPPED

Chop the onions and garlic and sauté gently in the olive oil until soft. Add the potatoes and continue cooking with the lid on, stirring from time to time to avoid browning. If necessary, add more oil.

When the potatoes are starting to soften, add the stock or water.

215

Give it a good stir, and then simmer for half an hour until the potatoes are cooked through. Then blend, sieve or break down the potatoes with a masher. Season. Finally, stir in the chopped coriander. Trickle with olive oil and and serve with bread.

ROAST BELLY OF PORK WITH FRISÉE LETTUCE AND PRUNES

1.4kg (3lb) BELLY OF PORK ON THE BONE
OIL
SALT AND FRESHLY GROUND BLACK PEPPER
18 NEW POTATOES, PARBOILED AND ROUGHLY CHOPPED
1 BUNCH OF OREGANO, ROUGHLY CHOPPED

1 CURLY ENDIVE/FRISÉE LETTUCE
VINAIGRETTE
18 PRUNES, SOAKED IN A LIGHT SYRUP WITH A LITTLE BRANDY (OPTIONAL)

Be nice to your butcher, and ask him to cut the pork into 18 pieces – 6 slices one way, and 3 the other way through the bone.

Blanch in boiling salted water for 10 minutes. Drain, and coat with a little oil, salt and pepper.

Roast in a tin in a medium-hot oven for 2 hours. Add the potatoes and oregano and cook for a further 20 minutes.

Toss the frisée in vinaigrette and arrange on the plates. Throw everything else on top, including all the bits from the pan, but leaving behind the oil.

ROASTED NUT TART WITH CHOCOLATE SAUCE

FOR THE PASTRY

125g (4oz) UNSALTED BUTTER
50g (2oz) ICING SUGAR
1 TEASPOON LEMON ZEST
75ml (2½fl oz) EGGS AND WATER MIXED TOGETHER, HALF AND HALF (1 EGG SHOULD BE ENOUGH)
225g (8oz) PLAIN FLOUR

Soften the butter to the extent that you can put a whisk through it.

Whisk in the icing sugar, zest, and then the egg mixture. It will curdle – don't worry.

Mix in the sieved flour, rubbing it in lightly with the tips of your fingers.

Form it into a ball, flatten it, wrap it in clingfilm and chill.

FOR THE NUT MIXTURE

50g (2oz) SOFT BUTTER
300g (10oz) MIXED WHOLE NUTS (125g 4oz FOR THE MIXTURE, 175g/6oz TO GO ON TOP)
A FEW GRATINGS OF NUTMEG
125g (4oz) SOFT BROWN SUGAR
2 EGGS
ICING SUGAR FOR DECORATION

Putting aside 175g (6oz) of the nuts (almonds, walnuts, hazelnuts, pine-nuts, pistachios, pecans), whizz the rest of the ingredients together in a food processor, or chop the nuts and mix by hand.

Preheat the oven to 180°C/350°F/gas 4. Line a 20cm (8in) tart tin with the pastry (you may not need all of it) and bake blind.

Fill with the nut mixture, and arrange the reserved whole nuts on top to cover it completely.

Lower the oven to 160°C/325°F/gas 3 and cook the tart until set – if the oven is too high, the nuts will burn instead of roasting. Dust with icing sugar using a fine sieve.

This is delicious with a chocolate sauce.

CHOCOLATE SAUCE

175ml (6fl oz) DOUBLE CREAM
3 TABLESPOONS GOLDEN SYRUP
200g (7oz) CASTER SUGAR
90g (3½oz) BITTER CHOCOLATE
25g (1oz) UNSALTED BUTTER
A FEW DROPS OF VANILLA ESSENCE

Heat the cream, syrup and sugar gently until soft. Add the chocolate and simmer until the sauce thickens (about 20 minutes), stirring all the while.

Remove from the heat and whisk in the butter bit by bit. Add vanilla essence to taste.

BRUCE POOLE
CHEZ BRUCE

Bruce Poole is serious and fierce. If he decides to do something, he'll do it – and do it properly. Fools are not suffered gladly. If, like me, you have a natural inclination towards ping-pong rather than rugger, if you go through life being puzzled and confused and ineffectual most of the time, Bruce Poole is an alarming person to meet. He makes categorical statements with little room for doubt or ambiguity. 'Fruit fools are made up of fruit and cream. That's *it*. Anything else is a load of bollocks.' And when it comes to whipping the cream, you have to be careful. If you whip it too stiffly: 'You're fucked and you're history.' He was contemptuous of my limp-wristed reluctance to include a recipe for calves' brains and very suspicious (with good reason) of much of the costing of these recipes. 'I know *for a fact* that when I make lemon tart, it costs a quid a portion . . .'

But I wish I'd had a tape recorder running. It was impossible to keep pace with the mass of information that poured out of him as he started to describe how to go about cooking the meal. He's worked at the Square with Philip Howard and he opened Chez Max with the twins Max and Marc Renzland. He's also one of these very sensible people who believe cooking has quite a lot to do with simple things tasting good. Hence his choice of poule au pot, 'a cheap, old-fashioned and wonderful thing', with a béarnaise sauce – 'the best all-purpose sauce in the world'.

POT DE PROVENCE

A small, very rich combination of tomato salad, tapenade and egg mayonnaise. It's served in baby ramekins or glass dishes with toast.

FOR THE TOMATO SALAD

10 TOMATOES
3 SHALLOTS
2 TABLESPOONS OLIVE OIL
6 BASIL LEAVES, CHOPPED
SALT AND FRESHLY GROUND
BLACK PEPPER

Blanch the tomatoes for seconds in boiling water, then peel and seed them and finely dice the flesh. Chop the shallots so finely they're almost minced, mix with the tomatoes and dress with the olive oil and chopped basil. Season.

FOR THE TAPENADE

36 STONED BLACK OLIVES
(BIG FAT JUICY ONES)
1 TABLESPOON CAPERS
6 ANCHOVY FILLETS
2 CLOVES GARLIC
OLIVE OIL

Blitz the olives, capers, anchovies and garlic in a blender and then trickle in olive oil to make a smooth tapenade paste.

FOR THE EGG MAYONNAISE

300ml (½ PINT) FRESH MAYONNAISE
6 HARD-BOILED EGGS
SALT AND FRESHLY GROUND
BLACK PEPPER
A SQUEEZE OF LEMON JUICE

Blend all the ingredients together.

Spoon a little tapenade into the base of each small ramekin dish. Then a layer of tomatoes, and then the egg mayonnaise on top. You eat it with a teaspoon, and serve with toast and any ice-cold baby radishes you happen to have in the fridge.

POULE AU POT

1½ CHICKENS
(OR 1 CHICKEN AND
A COUPLE OF LEGS)
FRESH THYME
1 BAY LEAF
PARSLEY STALKS IF
YOU HAVE THEM
A FEW PEPPERCORNS
½ HEAD OF GARLIC,
SLICED ACROSS

2 LEEKS
3 CELERY STALKS
6 CARROTS
½ SMALL SAVOY
CABBAGE
6 MEDIUM
POTATOES, PEELED
AND CUT INTO
HEALTHY CHUNKS

Place the chicken in a casserole with water to cover, add the herbs, peppercorns and garlic, bring to the boil and simmer for an hour, adding the vegetables as you go along so everything is cooked at the same time without the vegetables turning to soggy mush. One way of doing it – the best way – is to be mildly extravagant. Poach the chicken for 45 minutes with the herbs and the leeks, carrots and celery. Then discard the vegetables – which have gone into flavouring the broth – and replace with fresh leeks, carrots and celery about 15 minutes before the end. (Mind you, it's not *that* extravagant.) You can also add the potatoes at this point, and the Savoy cabbage goes in just before serving.

Serve in large soup bowls, because you want it to be soupy and brothy.

FOR THE SAUCE BÉARNAISE

375g (12 oz) BUTTER
4 SHALLOTS,
EXCEEDINGLY FINELY
CHOPPED
½ WINEGLASS OF
WHITE WINE
1 TABLESPOON
WHITE WINE
VINEGAR
(TARRAGON
VINEGAR IS PERFECT)
5 EGG YOLKS
1 LARGE BUNCH OF
FRESH TARRAGON,
CHOPPED
1 TABLESPOON
PARSLEY

Leave the butter somewhere warm so that it melts gradually for an hour or so, and it will clarify of its own accord, with all the buttermilk sinking to the bottom. This is a Very Good Thing, because – although it isn't essential to use clarified butter in the sauce – it's better because the sauce, sans buttermilk, will be thicker. And because the chicken casserole is wet and brothy, you want a thick sauce to go with it.

Meanwhile, cook the shallots, the wine and vinegar down to a glaze. Allow to cool slightly, and then – on a very low flame – beat in the egg yolks. First they'll go pale and then they'll thicken up. If you see any steam, add a few drops of cold water. Then gradually beat in the butter, and finally add the tarragon and parsley. You should be able to taste the vinegar. If you can't, add a drop of lemon juice. This is another of these deeply civilised sauces that will keep warm quite happily for an hour, which makes serving everything together a doddle.

Note: This recipe serves 6. If you want to make less, the proportions are 3 egg yolks to 250g (8oz) of butter.

RHUBARB FOOL

The basic method is the same whether you're using rhubarb, gooseberry, peaches or apricots. The only thing that varies is the method you use and the time it takes to cook the fruit. Peaches, for example, you'd poach. Gooseberries would be cooked the same way as rhubarb, but for much less time, and so on . . .

1kg (2¼lb) RHUBARB	JUICE AND ZEST OF 5 ORANGES
350g (12oz) SUGAR (THE PROPORTIONS ARE APPROXIMATELY ONE THIRD SUGAR TO RHUBARB)	600 ml (1 PINT) DOUBLE CREAM 2 TABLESPOONS CASTER SUGAR

Cut the rhubarb into 2.5cm (1in) pieces and put in a baking dish with the sugar and the juice and zest of the oranges. Cover with foil and bake in a low oven 150°C/300°F gas 2 for an hour. Let it cool and then drain, reserving the liquor.

Whip up the cream with the sugar, but not too stiffly. ('Whisk fairly thickly, but not too thickly.')

Blitz half the rhubarb in a blender with some of the liquor – not all, because otherwise you'll end up with a runny mess. What you want is a thick purée. Fold that into the whipped cream, stir in the rest of rhubarb and pour into glasses.

In a perfect world, serve with homemade shortbread.

ADAM ROBINSON
THE BRACKENBURY

Meeting Adam Robinson at 9.30 am on a wet Monday morning in Acton in the middle of February was hugely entertaining. He's a sort of Mick Jagger figure without attitude. Mick Jagger struts, Adam Robinson laughs. And they both dropped out of the London School of Economics.

But there the similarity ends. Adam Robinson went to Sandhurst but reckoned the two days he spent there was just about the right length of time to be in the army. And I doubt Mick Jagger's parents ever encouraged him towards a military career. From there – via a spell at the LSE, time out lurking in a squat and a couple of years driving around Latin America – he learned to cook.

In those days, in the early 1980s, it was unusual to be white and middle-class and want to work for £60 a week as an apprentice in a kitchen. It was regarded with the same sort of suspicion that would greet an old Etonian wanting to be a hairdresser. But he ended up working with Alistair Little, Rowley Leigh, the Roux brothers and Kenneth Lo, and cooked his way round a variety of kitchens in France.

He now has two restaurants: the Chiswick, 'catering to the good burghers of Chiswick. The sort of the people who'd live in Holland Park if they could afford to', and the Brackenbury, very much a local restaurant, catering to 'somewhat lesser burghers. Mostly from the BBC.'

BROCCOLI WITH ANCHOVY DRESSING

1.4kg (3lb) SPROUTING BROCCOLI (OR ORDINARY BROCCOLI)	2 HEADS OF CHICORY 50g (2oz) PARMESAN CHEESE

FOR THE DRESSING

50g (2oz) ANCHOVY FILLETS	½ TABLESPOON DIJON MUSTARD
1 GARLIC CLOVE	½ TABLESPOON RED WINE VINEGAR
½ TABLESPOON FRESH BASIL	¼ CHOPPED RED OR GREEN CHILLI
½ TEASPOON FRESH THYME	120ml (4fl oz) OLIVE OIL

Put all the dressing ingredients into a whizzer, adding the olive oil a dribble at a time, emulsifying as though making mayonnaise.

Steam the broccoli, mix with the chicory and turn in the dressing. Garnish with shavings of Parmesan on top.

SMOKED HADDOCK WITH POACHED EGG AND A BUTTER SAUCE

('I can give you something more poncy if you like,' he offered. 'But this is delicious. I love it. I do it a lot. The English demean it by calling it nursery food. The French are much more sensible – they call it *cuisine grand-mère*, which makes it sound much more appetising.')

1kg (2¼lb) SMOKED WHITE (UNDYED) HADDOCK (175g/6oz PER PERSON)	MILK AND WATER FOR POACHING (HALF AND HALF) 6 EGGS

FOR THE SAUCE

2 LARGE SHALLOTS, FINELY CHOPPED
250g (8oz) BUTTER
1 WINEGLASS WHITE WINE
½ WINEGLASS WATER

Sweat the shallots in a little butter. Add the wine and reduce it to zilch. Add ¼ of a wineglass of water and, again, reduce it to nothing. This kills the acidity in the wine. Add another dribble of water, then slowly whisk in 250g (8oz) of butter a bit at a time over a low heat.

Poach the eggs for 3 minutes in simmering water that has a dribble of vinegar in it to stop the egg whites shooting all over the place. (I asked him if there was any way of getting rid of the not-very-nice smell of hot vinegar. 'Sure,' he said. 'Buy an extraction unit.') Meanwhile, poach the haddock in milk and water for roughly the same amount of time as it takes to cook the eggs. Or if you're not worried about a bit of shooting egg white, you can poach the eggs in the same pan as the haddock.

Serve the egg on top of the haddock – in a perfect world, on a bed of spinach – surrounded by the butter sauce.

STEAMED GINGER PUDDING WITH CRÈME ANGLAISE (AKA CUSTARD)

125g (4oz) FLOUR
125g (4oz) FRESH BREADCRUMBS
125g (4oz) VEGETABLE SUET
1 TEASPOON MIXED SPICE
1½ DESSERTSPOONS BAKING POWER
A PINCH OF SALT
480ml (15fl oz) MILK
1½ EGGS (ONE AND A HALF EGGS.
GIVE THE OTHER HALF TO THE CAT)
250g (9oz) STEM GINGER, FINELY CHOPPED (RETAIN THE GINGER SYRUP)
350g (12oz) GOLDEN SYRUP, PLUS AN EXTRA 1cm (½in) OF SYRUP FOR THE BOTTOM OF THE BASIN

Mix together all the dry ingredients in a bowl, and all the wet ingredients in another bowl.

Make a well in the middle of the dry stuff, mix in the wet ingredients and stir to a sludge. Turn out into a large, well-buttered pudding basin with 1cm (½in) of syrup in the bottom, cover with foil and steam for 2 hours.

FOR THE CRÈME ANGLAISE

4 EGG YOLKS
125g (4oz) SUGAR
600ml (1 PINT) MILK
½ VANILLA POD

Whisk the egg yolks and the sugar in a bowl. Pour over the boiling milk which has been infusing with the vanilla pod. Back into the pan and cook gently, making sure you don't scramble the eggs. ('That's 83 degrees for two minutes,' says Robinson. 'If anyone insists on being anal about it.')

227

GUNTHER SCHLENDER

My closest friend was a German called Harald. 'Harald' with an 'a'. We lived together for two years in a house that was collapsing very picturesquely behind the Edgware Road. I cooked and he filled the place with people. Harald went on to open an art gallery in Hamburg, until at five o'clock one morning he chose a secluded spot down by the lake and shot himself. One of the many things he left me was a strong prejudice in favour of Germans.

I originally wrote to Gunther Schlender at his own restaurant, the Rue St Jacques in Charlotte Street. My letter was returned — the restaurant had gone bust. I finally caught up with him at the Roof Kitchen of the Royal Garden Hotel in Kensington. He hadn't received any of my letters, but immediately agreed to meet me. 'You see,' I thought to myself. 'You see. *Another* kindly German.'

Not surprisingly, the inside of a posh hotel looks very different to the derelict squalor of streets around Tottenham. I parked my bike in the bowels of the building, down a ramp, through plastic swing doors where all the luggage was stored. I folded away my nasty yellow anorak, straightened my tie, and then padded across the foyer feeling distinctly sheepish. I lurked by the desk. The guy behind the desk asked the American standing beside me if he could help. The American indicated that I was first. No, please, I said. Please. Go ahead. I mean, for God's sake, I'm not even supposed to be here. I mean, you're paying. I busied myself reading a sign advertising the New Year Gourmet Dinner with all the Olde Englishe trimmings in the Roof Kitchen: £140 a head. A bargain, considering it included a complimentary cocktail.

The Roof Kitchen restaurant was on the tenth floor, and the view across parks and gardens was green and restful. From up there, London looked very peaceful and still. There were a couple of

228

Americans dawdling over their coffee, otherwise the restaurant was empty.

Gunther Schlender came out. Very neat. Very clean. All starch and a white cravat. Ascetic almost, like a slightly mournful dentist.

'What a wonderful view across London,' I said.

'Enjoy it while you can – it's not going to be around much longer. The hotel has structural problems. It's being closed down and everybody has been given notice.' He smiled sadly. 'It hasn't been a good year.'

COURGETTE AND LETTUCE SOUP

450g (1lb) COURGETTES
2 LETTUCES – ANYTHING BUT ICEBERG, WHICH HAS NEITHER TASTE NOR COLOUR
1 ONION, SLICED
225g (8oz) POTATO, DICED
BUTTER
½ BAY LEAF
1 LITRE (1¾ PINTS) CHICKEN STOCK
SALT AND FRESHLY GROUND BLACK PEPPER
LEMON JUICE
CREAM

Roughly chop the courgettes, the lettuce, the onion and the potatoes, and sweat them all together in a little butter with the ½ bay leaf. Season. Add the chicken stock, bring to the boil and simmer until the vegetables are soft. Liquidise, strain and finish with a squeeze of lemon juice and a dash of cream.

CHICKEN STIR-FRY

I've been doing awful things to stir-fries for years. The vegetables end up flabby, sloshing around in a salty, over-spiced sauce. Herein lies the solution.

229

3 SKINNED CHICKEN	2 GARLIC CLOVES,
BREASTS	CHOPPED
2 TABLESPOONS	2 CHILLIES, CRUSHED
SESAME OIL	5cm (2in) GINGER
2 TABLESPOONS	FRESHLY GROUND
SOY SAUCE	BLACK PEPPER

Any cheap selection of vegetables – turnips, swede, flowerets of cauliflower, carrots, beans, mangetout, strips of pepper; literally, anything in the market that's fresh and cheap

Cut the chicken into 'batons' – slim fingers rather than slivers – and marinate them for a couple of hours with the sesame oil, garlic, chillies, peeled ginger and ground pepper. The marinade should coat the chicken – it shouldn't be drowning in it.

Blanch the vegetables and refresh them under the cold tap.

Stir-fry the chicken in a tablespoon of sesame oil seasoned with salt and pepper until just cooked. Remove and keep warm. Then do the same thing with the vegetables.

Mix the soy sauce and whatever liquid is left behind from stir-frying the vegetables with an extra dash of sesame oil, then cook out with a nugget of butter and a squeeze of lemon. This will provide a glistening of sauce. Serve with rice.

THE RICE

1 ONION, FINELY	A LITTLE FINELY
CHOPPED	DICED CHILLI
A KNOB OF BUTTER	2.5cm (1in) FRESH
3 CUPS EASY-COOK	GINGER, PEELED AND
RICE	CHOPPED
4½ CUPS OF WATER	1 BAY LEAF
(THE RATIO IS 1 CUP	LOTS OF SALT AND
RICE TO 1½ CUPS	FRESHLY GROUND
WATER)	BLACK PEPPER

Sauté the onion in the butter until soft but not brown. Then add everything else and cook the whole lot in a medium oven for 20 minutes. You'll need to stir it once.

('My mother,' says Schlender, 'used to cook the rice on top of the stove for five minutes, then cover it tightly and leave it in a feather bed for half an hour.')

APPLE PIES MADE WITH FILO PASTRY

When it comes to serving, it's easier to deal with individual apple pies than one big one.

1 PACKET FILO PASTRY	A HINT OF CLOVE
900g (2lb) APPLES, PEELED, CORED AND WELL CHOPPED	LEMON JUICE TO TASTE
SUGAR TO TASTE	MELTED BUTTER, TO BRUSH
A PINCH OF NUTMEG AND CINNAMON	REDCURRANTS AND MINT LEAVES TO GARNISH (OPTIONAL)

Preheat the oven to 190°C/375°F/gas 5.

Line individual pie dishes with four squares of pastry – each square at a slight angle to the other to create a star effect, and allowing enough pastry to flap over the sides so that it can be turned over to form a lid.

Mix the apples with sugar, cinnamon, nutmeg, a little bit of clove and the lemon juice. Place some mixture in the centre of each pie dish and fold over the pastry, pinching it in the middle so you end up with what looks like a little sack or parcel of apple pie. Brush with melted butter.

Bake in the preheated oven for 15 minutes or until crisp and golden.

Dust with icing sugar and place on a thin pool of crème anglaise, (see page 227), garnished with a few redcurrants and a mint leaf.

SEBASTIAN SNOW
SNOWS ON THE GREEN

Honesty isn't a word that one would expect to hear over and over again in terms of food. A restaurant, after all, isn't a church. But it's a word that keeps cropping up in certain kitchens, and they all seem to be kitchens with a number of things in common. The chefs work cruel hours with enormous enthusiasm. The basic ingredients are always fresh and mostly local. The presentation is unfussy, the prices are sensible and the place is packed.

Sebastian Snow – the chef/proprietor of Snows on the Green at the bottom of the Shepherd's Bush Road – looks more like a male model than a chef. He isn't professionally trained although his mother is Italian – which is a bit like saying that a person may not have any money but their family are Rothschilds. And quite apart from anything else, he showed me the definitive way to make mashed potato, which is the main justification for the existence of this book.

Here is an honest chef if ever there was one.

MUTTON SOUP AND GRATIN

Like French onion soup, this isn't a delicate dish. But it's enormously friendly and heart-warming – a perfect meal on an icy day.

1 SHOULDER OF MUTTON, TRIMMED OF FAT AND STUDDED WITH ROSEMARY, THYME AND GARLIC ANYTHING YOU'VE GOT IN THE WAY OF ONIONS, CARROTS, LEEKS, CELERY, CELERIAC, TOMATOES, CABBAGE OR OTHER WINTER VEGETABLES
1 TABLESPOON SUGAR
SALT AND FRESHLY GROUND BLACK PEPPER
1 TABLESPOON GREMOLATA (OPTIONAL)

– A FINELY CHOPPED MIXTURE OF PARSLEY, LEMON ZEST AND GARLIC
1 EGG PER 600ml (1 PINT) OF SOUP (OPTIONAL)
1 LOAF OF STALE BREAD – A BAGUETTE WOULD BE IDEAL
GARLIC CLOVES
6 LEEKS (OPTIONAL)
175g (6oz) CHEESE (PARMESAN, PECORINO, GRUYÈRE – IF YOU'VE GOT A BIT OF OLD MOUSETRAP, THAT'S FINE)
BUTTER
CHOPPED PARSLEY

This is a two-in-one dish – a bowl of broth and a baked gratin. You can have the soup as a starter, and serve the gratin with a salad for the main course. Or you can cut out squares of the gratin and place one in each bowl of soup. Personally, I opt for the soup first and the gratin and salad as a main course, largely because I'm not overly fond of the soft texture of the gratin floating around in the soup.

Shoulder of mutton, or even lamb, is very cheap these days. Put the meat and all the vegetables into a very large saucepan, add the sugar, cover with water, bring to the boil and simmer for 4 hours, skimming off the scum from time to time, by which time the meat will be falling off the bone. Strain the stock, reduce by a third, remove the fat, correct the seasoning and there's your soup. Add a teaspoon of gremolata to each bowl; it gives a wonderful aromatic freshness.

To clarify the soup . . . Well, why not? It's all good clean fun. One egg white and one crushed egg shell for each pint of liquid. As the soup gradually heats, whisk. Stop whisking just before the soup threatens to boil. Remove from the heat, and when a crust has started to form, simmer again for 45 minutes. Sieve carefully through a colander lined with wet muslin. There you are, you see. Couldn't be easier.

For the gratin: take the meat off the shoulder of lamb and chop finely. Slice the bread thinly and rub with garlic, then toast. Chop the leeks into matchsticks and boil them in a little water for a couple of minutes. Slice the cheese.

To assemble: rub a small roasting tray with butter and garlic. Put a layer of toast to cover the bottom. Then a layer of meat, a layer of leeks, a layer of cheese, another layer of toast, and so on. The top layer should be toast with grated cheese. Pour over two small ladles of broth to moisten, and bake in a medium oven for half an hour or so until the top is golden. Scatter with finely chopped parsley.

POACHED ROE ON TOAST

18 HERRING ROES	A SQUEEZE OF
120ml (4fl oz)	ANCHOVY ESSENCE
REDUCED	SALT AND
FISH STOCK	FRESHLY GROUND
120ml (4fl oz)	BLACK PEPPER
DOUBLE CREAM	TOAST
	CHOPPED PARSLEY

Poach the herring roe in the stock and the cream with a little anchovy essence for 2 or 3 minutes and season to taste. Pile on to hot, crusty toast with a scattering of finely chopped parsley and serve immediately.

MACKEREL FRIED WITH CARAMELISED APPLES, AND THOSE ASTONISHING MASHED POTATOES

Deceptively simple, but a wonderful way of dealing with this grossly undervalued fish. The apples serve to cut through the oiliness of the mackerel.

6 MACKEREL   225g (8oz) WHITE
1 TABLESPOON   SUGAR
FLOUR   A FEW KNOBS OF
6 COOKING APPLES   BUTTER

FOR THE MASHED POTATOES

900g (2lb) POTATOES
500ml (16fl oz) HOT MILK
2 TABLESPOONS BUTTER
SALT AND FRESHLY GROUND
BLACK PEPPER

Ask the fishmonger to fillet the mackerel for you. Lightly dust with flour, fry slowly (skin-side down first) in butter until they colour to a deep golden-brown, then turn. Peel and slice the apples into wedges, toss in sugar and cook in the same pan as the mackerel. When the apples start to brown, add a knob of butter, which softens the sugar and stops it becoming bitter. In all, they should cook for 5 minutes or so.

For the mashed potatoes: peel, boil and drain the potatoes. Put them through a mouli, thence into a liquidiser with the hot milk and butter for 5 seconds. (For gawd's sake be careful. If you liquidise for too long, you end up with glue.) Adjust the seasoning. Undreamt of smoothness.

PAN-FRIED HERRING WITH MUSTARD SAUCE

6 HERRINGS
1 TABLESPOON FLOUR
A KNOB OF BUTTER

FOR THE SAUCE

900g (2lb) FISH BONES, FREE FROM YOUR FRIENDLY NEIGHBOURHOOD FISHMONGER
1 ONION, CHOPPED
1 CELERY STALK, CHOPPED
1 LEEK, CHOPPED
1 TEASPOON FRESH OR DRIED THYME
1 BAY LEAF
1 WINEGLASS WHITE WINE
4 TABLESPOONS DOUBLE CREAM
2 TABLESPOONS DIJON MUSTARD

Cook the herrings in exactly the same way as the mackerel in the previous recipe: ask your fishmonger to fillet them, lightly dust the herring fillets with flour, and fry slowly in butter (skin-side down first) then turn.

To make the mustard sauce, first make a fish stock. Soften the vegetables in a little butter. Add them to the fishbones, herbs and wine and 1.2 litres (2 pints) of water. Bring to the boil and simmer for 25 minutes. Strain, then reduce the stock to an espresso cup. Add cream and Dijon mustard to taste, heat through gently and season.

Again, serve with the famous mashed potatoes and some spinach.

236

SALMON LASAGNE WITH A SORREL SAUCE

Salmon is cheaper than cod. Hallelujah. The only people who shouldn't try to make this fiendishly attractive dish are those incapable of wrapping any sort of parcel, since each portion of the salmon lasagne is assembled individually.

900g (2lb) SPINACH
1 PACKET OF LASAGNE
900g (2lb) FILLET OF SALMON
900g (2lb) TOMATOES, BLANCHED, SKINNED AND SEEDED

Lightly steam the spinach.

Cook the lasagne.

Slice the raw fillets of salmon in half horizontally to make them thinner.

Assemble each portion on a square of clingfilm. First a layer of lasagne cut to the size of the salmon, then a layer of salmon, a layer of spinach, a layer of tomatoes, a second layer of salmon etc. There are three pieces of lasagne and two layers of salmon to each portion. Season each layer. Then wrap the clingfilm round each portion and lower into a tray of simmering water for 10 minutes.

The sorrel sauce is made in exactly the same way as the mustard sauce (see above), simply substituting chopped sorrel for mustard.

CHARLOTTE CLEMENTINES

8 SLICES OF WHITE BREAD
50g (2oz) BUTTER
12 CLEMENTINES
75g (3oz) SUGAR

Fry the bread in the butter, both sides, cut off the crusts and roll out thinly while still warm. Cut into fingers, leaving a circle for the top and bottom of each small ramekin dish. The fingers of fried bread around the sides should overlap each other.

Peel the clementines, separate the segments and caramelise them in the sugar for a minute and a half, add a little butter and pack tightly into the ramekin dishes and seal with a lid of fried bread.

Cover each dish tightly with tin foil and steam for half an hour in a tray of water in a medium oven – the water should reach half-way up the side of the dishes.

Turn out each one, put them under the grill to crisp them, and serve with crème anglaise (see page 227).

Alphabetical List of Restaurants

Abdel and Frances Boukraa
Adam's Café
77 Askew Road
London W12 9AH
Tel. 0181 743 0572

Mrs Atalla
Al Bustan
27 Motcomb Street
London SW1X 8JU
Tel. 0171 235 8277

Vincenzo Borgonzolo
Al San Vincenzo
30 Connaught Street
London W2 2AF
Tel. 0171 262 9623

Mrs Priyanu
Bedlington Café
24 Fauconberg Road
London W4 3JY
Tel. 0181 994 1965

Philippe Blaise
Belgo Noord
72 Chalk Farm Road
London NW1 8AN
Tel. 0171 267 0718

Maddalena Bonino
Bertorelli's
44A Floral Street
London WC2E 9DA
Tel. 0171 836 3969

Adam Robinson
Brackenbury
129–131 Brackenbury Road
London W6 0BQ
Tel. 0181 748 0107

Nigel Davis
Brasserie St Quentin
243 Brompton Road
London SW3 2EP
Tel. 0171 581 5131

Gary Pavitt
Charco's
1 Bray Place
London SW3 3LL
Tel. 0171 584 0765

Mary Healey
Cherry Orchard
241 Globe Road
London E2 0JE
Tel. 0181 980 6678

Bruce Poole
Chez Bruce
2 Bellevue Road
London SW17 7EG
Tel. 0181 672 0114

Richard Walton
Chez Moi
1 Addison Avenue
London W11 4QS
Tel. 0171 603 8267

Giancarlo Moeri
Como Lario
22 Holbein Place
London SW1W 8NL
Tel. 0171 730 2954

Aurelio Spagnuolo
Del Buongustaio
283 Putney Bridge Road
London SW15 2PT
Tel. 0181 780 9361
& **Osteria Antica Bologna**
23 Northcote Road
London SW11 ING
Tel. 0171 978 4711

Matthew Fanthorpe
dell' Ugo
56 Frith Street
London W1V 5TA
Tel. 0171 734 8300

David Eyre
Eagle
159 Farringdon Road
London ECIR 3AL
Tel. 0171 837 1353

Paul Bloxham
Fire Station
150 Waterloo Road
London SE1 8SB
Tel. 0171 620 2226

Laszlo Holecz
Gay Hussar
2 Greek Street
London WIV 6NB
Tel. 0171 437 0973

Bryan Webb
Hilaire
68 Old Brompton Rd.
London SW7 3LQ
Tel. 0171 584 8993

Eric Crouillère-Chavot
Interlude de Chavot
5 Charlotte Street
London W1P 1HD
Tel. 0171 637 0222

Des McDonald
Ivy
1 West Street
London WC2H 9NE
Tel. 0171 834 4751

Rowley Leigh
Kensington Place
201 Kensington Church Street
London W8 7LX
Tel. 0171 727 3184

Alain Perdrix
L'Aventure
3 Blenheim Terrace
London NW8 0EO
Tel. 0171 624 6232

Jean-Luc Morcellet
La Dordogne
5 Devonshire Road
London W4 2EU
Tel. 0181 747 1836

Amanda Pritchett
Lansdowne
90 Gloucester Avenue
London NW1 8HX
Tel. 0171 483 0409

Laurent Farrugia
Laurent's
428 Finchley Road
London NW2 2HY
Tel. 0171 794 3603

Tony Howorth
Le Café du Jardin
28 Wellington Street
Covent Garden
London WC2E 7BD
Tel. 0171 836 8769

Mark Hix and Tim Hughes
Le Caprice
Arlington House
Arlington Street
London SW1A 1RT
Tel. 0171 629 2239

Gillian Enthoven
Le Mesurier
113 Old Street
London EC1V 9JR
Tel. 0171 251 8117

Max Renzland
Le Petit Max
97A High Street
Hampton Wick
London KT2 5NB
Tel. 0181 977 0236

Peter Kromberg
Le Soufflé
Inter Continental Hotel
1 Hamilton Place
London W1V 0QY
Tel. 0171 409 3131

Gino Santin
L'Incontro
87 Pimlico Road
London SW1W 8PH
Tel. 0171 730 6327

Bruno Loubet
L'Odéon
65 Regent Street
London W1R 7HH
Tel. 0171 287 1400

Gilbert Rousset
Magno's
65A Long Acre
London WC2E 9JH
Tel. 0171 836 6077

Yousif Mukhayer
The Mandola
139 Westbourne Grove
London W11 2RS
Tel. 0171 229 4734

Thomas Benham
Monkeys
1 Cale Street
Chelsea Green
London SW3 3QT
Tel. 0171 352 4711

Mark Nathan and Gail Koerber
Museum Street Café
47 Museum Street
London WC1A 1LY
Tel. 0171 405 3211

Sandro Medda
Olivo
21 Eccleston Street
London SW1W 9LX
Tel. 0171 730 2505

Albert Clarke
192
192 Kensington Park Road
London W11 2ES
Tel. 0171 229 0482

Charles Fontaine
Quality Chop House
94 Farringdon Road
London EC1R 3EA
Tel. 0171 837 5093

David Philpott
Quincy's
675 Finchley Road
London NW2 2JP
Tel. 0171 794 8499

Hemant Desai
Sabras
263 High Road
Willesden Green
London NW10 2RX
Tel. 0181 459 0340

Fergus Henderson
St John
St John Street
London EC1M 4AY
Tel. 0171 251 0848

Richard Corrigan
Searcy's Brasserie
2nd Floor, Barbican Centre
Silk Street
London EC2Y 8DS
Tel. 0171 588 3008

Sebastian Snow
Snows on the Green
166 Shepherd's Bush Road
London W6 7PB
Tel. 0171 603 2142

Philip Howard
The Square
32 King Street
London SW1W 6RJ
Tel. 0171 839 8787

Stephen Bull
Stephen Bull
5–7 Blandford Street
London WIH 3AA
Tel. 0171 486 9696
& **Fulham Road**
257–259 Fulham Road
London SW3 6HY
Tel. 0171 351 7823
& **Stephen Bull's Bistro**
71 St John Street
London EC1M 4AN
Tel. 0171 490 1750

Paul Hodgson
Waltons
121 Walton Street
London SW3 2HP
Tel. 0171 584 0204

INDEX